Raymond Duchamp-Villon

1876–1918

Introduction by George Heard Hamilton

Notes by William C. Agee

 Walker and Company, New York

FRONTISPIECE: Fig. 1   *Large Horse.* 1914. Bronze, 59 in. high. Collection Louis Carré

Library of Congress Catalog Card Number: 67-30378
Published simultaneously in Canada by The Ryerson Press, Toronto
Printed in the United States of America
Jacket designed by Joseph Bourke Del Valle
Book designed by Bert Clarke

PUBLISHED BY WALKER AND COMPANY,
A DIVISION OF WALKER PUBLISHING COMPANY, INC.,
IN ASSOCIATION WITH
M. KNOEDLER & CO. INC., NEW YORK

Acknowledgments

The Publishers and M. Knoedler and Company wish to express gratitude to the following people for helping with the preparation of this volume and the Duchamp-Villon exhibition held at M. Knoedler and Company from October 10 through November 4, 1967: Mr. Alfred H. Barr, Jr., M. Louis Carré, M. Bernard Dorival, Mr. Marcel Duchamp, Mme. de Grandry, Mr. Abram Lerner, Mlle. Chantal Maisonnier, and M. Antoine Mounier. Special thanks are due Mr. John Savacool for translating the French documents.

List of Lenders

Albright-Knox Art Gallery, Buffalo; The Art Gallery of Ontario, Toronto; The Art Institute of Chicago; Jacques Bon, Paris; Louis Carré, Paris; The Detroit Institute of Arts; Marcel Duchamp, New York; Madame Duvernoy, Paris; The Solomon R. Guggenheim Museum, New York; The Joseph H. Hirshhorn Collection, New York; Dr. Robert Jullien, Paris; Edgar Kaufmann, jr., New York; Munson-Williams-Proctor Institute, Utica, New York; Musée des Beaux-Arts, Rouen; Musée National d'Art Moderne, Paris; The Museum of Art, The Rhode Island School of Design, Providence; The Museum of Modern Art, New York; Niels Onstad, Los Angeles; Mr. and Mrs. Raymond Peter Pach, Canton, North Carolina; Mrs. Walter Pach (Nikifora N. Iliopoulos), New York; The Phillips Collection, Washington, D.C.; Mr. and Mrs. William Rand, New York; Mr. and Mrs. M. Riklis, New York; Mr. and Mrs. Francis Steegmuller, New York; Vincent Tovell, Toronto; Dr. von Munchhausen, Bonn; Williams College, Museum of Art, Williamstown, Massachusetts; Yale University Art Gallery, New Haven; Anonymous

The following works by Jacques Villon which relate to his brother, Raymond, are included in the exhibition:

Portrait of M. Duchamp. 1904. Pencil, 11¼ × 13¾ in. Private collection.
Torso of a Young Man. 1910. Pencil, 17¾ × 14¼ in. Private collection.
Portrait of Raymond Duchamp-Villon. 1911. Oil, 13½ × 10⁷⁄₁₆ in. Musée National d'Art Moderne, Paris.
Baudelaire. ca. 1920. Etching, 16⅜ × 11⅛ in. Collection Mr. and Mrs. Raymond Peter Pach.
Le grand dessinateur assis (The Large Seated Draftsman). 1935. Oil, 21¾ × 18 in. Collection Mr. and Mrs. Francis Steegmuller.

Contents

9

Fig. 2   *Torso of a Young
Man.* 1910. Bronze,
22 in. high. Collection
Mrs. Walter Pach
(Nikifora N. Iliopoulos)

Raymond Duchamp-Villon

*He holds in splendid balance the intellectual analysis of the period
in which he had such robust faith and the style which his instinct
and tradition opened up to him.*

WALTER PACH

In 1929, little more than a decade after Duchamp-Villon's death, Walter Pach chose as the epigraph for his introduction to the first American retrospective of the sculptor's work two stanzas from "Les Phares," the poem in which Baudelaire included among the great artists who had been "lighthouses" for humanity his friend and contemporary, Eugène Delacroix. Pach's intention was to suggest that Duchamp-Villon too had been *un phare* of modern times, one of the lights, as he wrote, "that man has kindled against the night around him." Thinking of his own friend who had been lost in the universal night, Pach expressed his affection for the man as well as his respect for the sculptor whose works he, more than most, had helped to make known here and abroad. We know now that Pach's claims were not exaggerated. Duchamp-Villon's reputation is secure with one work, the majestic and menacing *Horse* (fig. 1), begun in 1914, which must be acknowledged as a climactic monument and moment in the formal development of twentieth-century sculpture. In itself it is a lighthouse that has illuminated the experience of sculpture in modern times.

The present epigraph—it was the last sentence in Pach's short statement of 1929—was not chosen to reassert Duchamp-Villon's position in the history of modern art, but to suggest that we still have an obligation to see this sculpture as a whole, rather than in a single example. The sensitive phrases of one of our earliest champions of modern art should encourage us to see how Duchamp-Villon held the complementary and conflicting claims of intellect and instinct in a splendid but uneasy balance between his appreciation of traditional concepts of French style and his awareness of the character of a truly modern art.

Raymond Duchamp-Villon, born in 1876, was the second of three brothers whose achievements have been central not only to French art but to the international movement as well. His older brother, Jacques Villon, born in 1875, studied law until he realized that his true talent lay in drawing and painting. For many years his illustrations for Parisian journals were inferior to those of Toulouse-Lautrec and Steinlen only to the degree that his touch was delicate where theirs was powerful; his insight gently ironical where theirs was more socially critical. In his paintings he had formulated by 1912 his own version of Cubism, and he had become the intellectual leader of a group of friends and artists who met at his studio in Puteaux across the Seine to the west of Paris. Among those who participated in their discussions were Fernand Léger, Albert Gleizes and Jean Metzinger, Juan Gris, Alexander Archipenko, and the youngest Duchamp brother,

Marcel, born in 1887. Together they arranged their own demonstration of the new painting and sculpture at their Salon de la Section d'Or, held in Paris in October 1912. In one sense the exhibition represented a gathering of forces against the increasing prestige of Picasso and Braque, the "Cubists of Montmartre." In another it proved that Cubism was no one's exclusive invention but rather a mode of vision, increasingly abstract and analytical, perhaps, in the work of the Puteaux artists, but capable of absorbing and resolving the artistic problems of many different personalities. Fifty-five years later it is easier to see that the work of Léger, Gris, Delaunay, and Villon, to mention only a few, was not only authentically Cubist but also of a quality that would have diminished Cubism by its absence. Perhaps this point may be made by reference to the painting that Marcel Duchamp contributed to the Section d'Or. His *Nude Descending a Staircase* (Philadelphia Museum of Art), that truly revolutionary visualization of space and motion, had been snubbed when he offered it to the Salon des Artistes Indépendants the previous March, yet when it was seen at the Armory Show in New York a year later it changed the course of modern art. Duchamp-Villon's contributions to the Section d'Or unfortunately cannot be identified; they are listed in the catalogue merely as "sculptures." But by then he had established the terms for the new sculpture through his persistent, even if not strictly Cubist, simplifications of the male nude (fig. 2) and the portrait bust (figs. 3 and 4).

If the productions of the Duchamp brothers were as various as their personalities were distinctive, a family resemblance can nevertheless be traced, at least through their attitudes toward art if not through their works. We might say that on the whole they were thinkers rather than doers, given to reflection on the nature of art and artists, and delighting as much in the formulation of problems as in their solution. Dismayed by the cupidity of the contemporary artistic marketplace they tended to stand slightly aside, confident that in the long run mind matters more than money. Thus Villon quietly supported long years of obscurity between the two World Wars until fame suddenly came to him after 1945 when a new generation, including many young Americans, discovered the luminous beauty of his translucent perspectives. Similarly Marcel Duchamp, who renounced his career as a practicing painter in 1918, deflected the course of Dada and Surrealism with no weapon weightier than his irony. What Duchamp-Villon would have done, or become, we cannot know. The unfinished *Horse* was the solitary climax to the pitifully few years allowed him, for he died at forty-two a few days before the Armistice of 1918.

Because Duchamp-Villon had studied medicine for three years before turning to sculpture, it is tempting to look in his work for evidence of a more than usually analytical perception of natural forms, but such a search will prove disappointing. Like every able young sculptor—he was twenty-two or so when he began—he first explored the dominant modes of the day. Self-taught, and so spared the routine of the schools, he flirted briefly with the fashions of 1900. The *Woman with Long Hair* (fig. 7) of about 1900 and the *Yvette Guilbert* (fig. 8) of about 1903 are typical of Art Nouveau. More important, and more interesting, is the group of portrait heads executed between 1904 and 1907 among which the bronze bust of his father (fig. 9) is a commendable exercise in the manner of Rodin. The luminous agitation of the surface which communicates the personal distinction of the sitter, no less than the twist of the head on the shoulders, shows that when Duchamp-Villon wished he could look closely at nature.

Of nearly the same year the terra-cotta head of an *Old Peasant* (fig. 15) offers a different solution, and one which was soon to become more important than any other. Here the planes of the face are smoothed tightly around the simpler volume of the head. Costume has been discarded and with it the restless profiles which accounted for so much of the personality of his father's bust. But there is no loss of character; on the contrary, it is revealed in his respect for appearances. The force of this head is the result of the powerfully sculptural understanding of the bulk of the nose, the eyes, the width of the mouth and upper lip, and the firm chin.

Other busts of the same period—those of his grandfather Emile Nicolle (fig. 12), an amateur engraver from whom the Duchamp brothers and sisters are thought to have inherited their artistic abilities, and the two versions of his sister Yvonne's portrait (figs. 16, 17)—show the same tendency toward a simplified mass scarcely distinguished by the projection of the features, and enclosed within quiet contours.

In 1902 Duchamp-Villon exhibited for the first time at the Salon of the Société Nationale des Beaux-Arts (the less conservative organization founded by Rodin and Puvis de Chavannes), and thereafter through 1908. In 1905 he became an associate member of the more adventurous Salon d'Automne, founded in 1903, where he exhibited annually until 1913 and served on various committees. Meanwhile in his own work he continued to alternate between the poles of open and closed form. A large *Torso* (fig. 14), a bronze cast of which is in the Musée National de l'Art Moderne in Paris, is anatomically the most searching of all his sculptures. The drooping body is mercilessly presented, but the purpose of the search remains obscure. From its slightly sagging posture one might expect a dramatic theme, somewhat as if this were a fragment of a female attendant for Rodin's anguished *Burghers of Calais*, as we know them in the preparatory nude studies. But within two years he abandoned such expressive treatment for the cool rhetoric of the *Seated Girl* of 1909 (fig. 21). The complexly coiled pose and the artificially elegant gestures recall similar work by other contemporary sculptors early on in their careers. Elie Nadelman and Gaston Lachaise, even Jacques Lipchitz who was to go so far in other directions, were momentarily attracted by the attenuated idealism of such subjects. Duchamp-Villon's figure is saved from banality only by what is unclassic about it, the clumsiness of the lower torso, especially when seen from the rear. This may be due not so much to the awkwardness of the self-taught sculptor feeling his way past such heavy shapes as to his admiration of Maillol whose formidable *Mediterranean* was first seen at the Salon d'Automne of 1905. From another

13

point of view, that exhibition might have confirmed Duchamp-Villon's interest in the possibility of a classic program for modern times, for there he would also have seen a small Ingres retrospective. The thought of Maillol is the more tantalizing because of another reference later on. Twenty years afterwards, in his memorial for Claude Debussy, Maillol perpetuated the mannered idealism of the *Seated Girl*, even to the gesture of the hand held stiffly at right angles to the wrist.

The next year Duchamp-Villon set himself a more difficult problem in the resolution of tradition with the new. The tight conjunction of form and subject in the *Pastorale* of 1910 (fig. 25), where the two figures are squeezed within the planes of the cubical block, resembles a Romanesque capital. It is perhaps less significant that the subject, which might be taken as Adam in pursuit of Eve, could be thought tangentially Biblical, than that such a theme may have been discussed at Puteaux. Marcel Duchamp's *Spring* of 1911, which survives in a small oil sketch and as the lowest layer of the epochal *Network of Stoppages* of 1914 (both in the Mary Sisler Collection, New York), contained a male and female nude, their bodies similarly treated as simplified and flattened planes.

It is the form, of course, more than the subject, that distinguishes *Pastorale* not only from all the other Parisian nudes of 1910, but even the "Adam" here from "Eve." Of the two the female figure proved the less sculpturally tractable. She reappeared the next year, standing upright, as the *Girl of the Wood* (fig. 29), but although the limbs and lower body are simpler and more abstract, more like Maillol one might almost say, they are still awkwardly contrasted with the naturalistic face and the fashionable "*belle poitrine.*" On the other hand, the male nude was to have an important future. He returns, seemingly later the same year, as the *Torso of a Young Man*, the first of Duchamp-Villon's sculptures to be recognized by his contemporaries as authentically "modern," and the first to remain so.

Despite the abbreviated arms and legs, the vigorous striding pose, which is almost identical with the figure in *Pastorale*, reveals its classic origin in such late antique works as the *Borghese Warrior* or, as William Agee observed, in the *Gladiator of Agassas*, used as an *écorché* at the École des Beaux-Arts. Yet if the *Torso of a Young Man* looks so far backwards, how can it be of its own time, and does it even look ahead to our own? Can it be considered, as some have thought, one of the first Cubist sculptures?

It is still difficult to define what can properly be called Cubist sculpture. The primary document—Picasso's *Head* of 1909—is Cubist in that the surface of the face and hair is broken into irregular facets meeting at such sharp angles that the basic volume of the head can scarcely be seen beneath them. The facets, however, are so obviously a translation into three dimensions of the broken planes of Picasso's paintings that the problem arises as to whether this is an essentially sculptural statement. Nor was the problem solved a few years later when Picasso and others, Lipchitz among them, restated the interpenetration of planes and the visual puns of Synthetic Cubist paintings in shallow reliefs. If Duchamp-Villon's *Torso* has anything to do with Picasso's Cubism, which

Fig. 3 *Baudelaire*. 1911. Bronze, 15¾ in. high. Collection, The Museum of Modern Art, New York. Alexander M. Bing Bequest

15

would be strange given the antipathy between Puteaux and Montmartre, it must be with such proto-Cubist images as Picasso's schematic paintings of male and female figures of 1908–09. A *Male Nude* of 1909 (Philadelphia Museum of Art) shows the same massive trunk, its muscular structure subsumed in a broad triangular plane, as in Duchamp-Villon's *Torso*. More provocative is the suggestion, in the turn of the body and its lunging stride, of the explicit movement of Boccioni's *Unique Forms of Continuity in Space* of 1913 and of the abstract energies which were to be compacted within Duchamp-Villon's own *Horse* the year after that.

The broad smooth planes of the *Torso* were an indication of what was to come, but Duchamp-Villon was not entirely done with the past. In the same year, 1910, he modeled the composition known as *Decorative Basin* (figs. 31, 32), literally a fountain basin, quite as suggestive of the utilitarian allegories of Art Nouveau, where similar figures wound their way across articles of ordinary use, as of Rodin on whose *Gates of Hell* Duchamp-Villon would have seen figures almost as summarily modeled as his own and whose emotional distress was also expressed by the contortion of the body and limbs. But perhaps the problem of psychological expression was the least of his concerns in *Decorative Basin*. If we may associate with it, perhaps even as deriving from it, a small plaster figure with raised arms which has lately come to light (fig. 59), we can see that the sculptor was moving rapidly toward more radical simplifications. The pose of a nude female figure with arms raised, as if arranging her hair, is as classically archetypical as the *Borghese Warrior*, but this figure suggests the more revolutionary revision of the classical prototype which Duchamp-Villon might have found in Picasso's *Demoiselles d'Avignon* of 1906–07, if indeed he could have seen it. Picasso's picture seems to have been hidden in his studio during these years, and what we may be watching here is rather a similar study of style, even of antiquity, a comparable search, like Picasso's, for forms, not subjects, that would be artistically expressive.

At the Salon of 1911 Duchamp-Villon presented his *Baudelaire* (fig. 3), a head whose formidable simplicity projects the image of the poet less as a man than as a disembodied intelligence. The contrast with Rodin's *Baudelaire* of 1898, also a posthumous evocation, has often been remarked. Both owe less to their author's study of contemporary photographs than to their conception of poetic genius. Rodin saw the face as a tremulous web stretched over the bones, Duchamp-Villon as a saturnine and introspective face dominated by the powerful sphere of the skull. That this image was the result of a sculptural as well as intellectual process is apparent in the earlier studies, in two bronzes which preserve the trace of his fingers searching for the principal form, and in a drawing where the features have already been treated as angular planes.

A similar process led to an even more remarkable result in the large bust of *Maggy* of 1911 (fig. 4). In an early study the surface still retains Rodinesque traces of the sculptor's tool while the tilt and turn of the head still convey much of the personality of the sitter, the wife of the poet and painter Georges Ribemont-Dessaignes. Below the

Fig. 4   *Maggy*. 1911.
Bronze, 29⅛ in. high.
Collection The Solomon
R. Guggenheim Museum,
New York

Fig. 5   *The Lovers*. 1913. Plaster, 27½ × 46 in. Collection, The Museum of Modern Art, New York

face the neck changes into an indefinite mass even less shapeless than the roughly modeled base with which Matisse terminated the last three versions of *Jeannette* of 1910–11. It is with the last of these, the familiar head from which he sliced away the abundant coiffure and brutally gouged the left eye and cheek, that Duchamp-Villon's may best be compared. Matisse's bust, which is visually disturbing even now, may still be the more radical, but Duchamp-Villon's has its surprises. It is even, if the word may be used, uglier, at least to the degree that the whole seems more a caricature and less a portrait, more savage in that it seems closer to primitive sculpture, to African Negro art whose plastic properties he otherwise seems to have ignored. Yet it is just those qualities that account for *Maggy's* unquestionable if ferocious power. From the first he had sensed in his sitter's face the expressive character of the wide thin mouth whose narrow upper lip he had already, in the small model, carried back in a sweeping plane as far as the cheekbone. He needed only to reinforce and strengthen the dominant nose, the protuberant eyes, and the cap of close-fitting hair to find the powerful formal harmonies of the final version. Here is a sculpture that can be compared only with Brancusi's work of the same period, such as *Mlle. Pogany*, also of 1912. And is not *Maggy's* throat, as strong as a tree trunk, like the cylindrical torso that Brancusi created later for his *Torso of a Young Man* of 1922?

The *Seated Woman* of 1914 (fig. 57) has long been better known than *Maggy*, but although two years later in time it is perhaps not essentially so progressive. Archipenko in the same year had pushed further beyond resemblance in the abstract conflict of his *Boxers (Struggle)*. Nevertheless, Duchamp-Villon's suppression of all details of hair, features, fingers, and toes, and his treatment of the separate parts of the body as interlocking ovoid shapes gave his figure such a "machine-turned" look that it has often been considered a primary instance of the influence of the machine aesthetic on modern sculpture. But, as in the *Torso of a Young Man* of four years before, the past was still at work just below the mechanically smooth surface, for one may have the feeling that the sculptor found his theme less in nature than in the unstable contrapposto of Michelangelo's *Virgin and Child* of the Medici Chapel.

Having mastered sculpture in the round, Duchamp-Villon turned to relief. The subject of his best-known work in this manner, *The Lovers* (figs. 51–54) of 1913, may once again have been suggested by Maillol whose commanding *Desire* of 1905–08, probably the most remarkable relief of the early twentieth century, shows a similar confrontation of crouching nudes. Duchamp-Villon, working on a smaller scale—his final version is almost as wide as Maillol's but only half as high—reversed the figures and twisted them into a more ecstatic, less architectonic pose. Their hands and feet no longer touch the edges of the rectangular frame as Maillol's do. Their arms, however, repeat with spacious gestures the curved outlines of the shallow depression in which they crouch, and their bodies have been reduced to little more than curved and triangular projections. In *The Lovers*, more than anywhere else until this time, could be seen

Duchamp-Villon's relationship with other members of the group of Puteaux. Here is a Cubist sculpture in the strict sense of the flattened figural style of his companions of the Section d'Or, especially of the paintings of Gleizes, Metzinger, and Jacques Villon. The second and final version (fig. 54) is both clearer and more abstract, and perhaps thereby more convincingly three-dimensional. In this he eliminated several redundant shapes, including the man's pincerlike feet and the conjoined forearms which tended to crowd the center.

In another subject, *The Small Dancers* of c. 1912 (fig. 45), he carried further the presentation of forms projecting in slight relief from within a shallow depression. The figures are simplified but still naturalistic and, like *The Lovers*, appear against a concave background. In the later state concavities have become convex so that the background emerges as a broad irregular ridge around the figures which, negatives of themselves as it were, are almost illegible. In what may possibly be a preliminary study (fig. 44), a plaster of the right-hand dancer, the configuration is more easily understood as a system of entirely abstract forms projecting in front of and behind the middle plane of the ground.

Duchamp-Villon's interest in abstraction had meanwhile led him to study architectural ornament. In 1910 he had been asked his opinion of the plan to remove Carpeaux's notable relief of *La Danse* from the facade of the Opéra to the Louvre in order to arrest its deterioration. In his reply, first published in *Gil Blas* in 1912, he stated his "meager formula" for monumental sculpture. "Seen from a distance," he wrote, it should "live as decoration through the harmony of volumes, planes, and lines," adding that the subject was "of little or no importance." This interest in an abstract or architectural sculpture appeared in the facade he designed in 1912 for a full-scale model of a private house to be erected at the Salon d'Automne of 1912. Because of space restrictions only the first story was actually erected in the Grand Palais. The interior consisted of a suite of rooms decorated under the direction of André Mare by several of the Puteaux artists, among them La Fresnaye, Léger, Metzinger, and Marie Laurencin. His own *Decorative Basin* was on one of the mantelpieces. Nicknamed the "Maison Cubiste," this imaginative attempt to create a new and comprehensive decorative style was on the whole unfavorably received by the critics and public. In the existing photograph the model looks more conventional than otherwise. The symmetrical disposition of the principal elements flanking a central motif of door, window, and crowning pediment follows the traditional *ordonnance* of an eighteenth-century town house. Only the geometrically faceted ornament around the doors and windows could be called Cubist, and then only because the angular shapes, now entirely abstract, resemble those in the reliefs of *The Lovers*.

This unstable conjunction of traditional architecture with a more daring sculptural ornament would also have been seen in a second project which Duchamp-Villon undertook for Walter Pach in the spring of 1914. They had met and become fast friends late

Fig. 6 *Seated Woman.*
1914 Bronze, 25¾ in.
high. Yale University
Art Gallery. Bequest of
Katherine S. Dreier for
the Collection of the
Société Anonyme

in 1912 when Pach, with Arthur B. Davies and Walt Kuhn, had come to Europe to select works of art for an international exhibition, the famous Armory Show, which they were planning to hold in New York the following spring. Duchamp-Villon sent his *Torso of a Young Man*, *Baudelaire*, the small *Dancers* and the model of the "Maison Cubiste." The second commission was for a series of academic buildings to be erected somewhere in Connecticut (strangely, neither the site nor the sponsor, a man named Chappell, have been identified). This time Duchamp-Villon looked to late medieval English architecture for a design no more nor less advanced and, to judge from a photograph of the plaster model of the dormitory, no more Cubist than the general run of early twentieth-century collegiate Gothic. Only the sculptural ornament could have been considered up-to-date. The bay window would have been decorated with cubistically geometrical compositions in low relief representing the planets on the upper band, the stars below, and the moon and moonlight on the lowest level, the whole, in his own words, symbolizing the heavens, an appropriate theme for a dormitory.

Shortly before then—in the early spring of 1914—he had decided that the decorative bas-reliefs should contain small figures of people or animals. It is tempting to think that the animals might have resembled those in four reliefs of 1913. One, the *Parrot*, was carved in oak (fig. 49). The other three—a dog, a cat, and two doves (figs. 48, 46–47, 50) —were cast in cement, then a novel material for sculpture but one that may have come to Duchamp-Villon's attention through his awareness of contemporary architecture and of Auguste Perret's work in reinforced concrete which he mentioned in his essay on the Eiffel Tower.

Each of the animals or birds, its body reduced like those of the *Lovers* to a sequence of angular ridges, is inscribed within an irregular circle. The reliefs have the additional characteristic that in each a bird's tail or animal's forepaw projects as a small oval shape beyond the circumference of the circle. Considered as self-sufficient works of art they are oddly ill-defined. Only the *Parrot*, its circular design set firmly against the square wooden panel, holds its place on a two-dimensional surface. If, on the other hand, the three cement reliefs were intended as architectural ornaments, the bold projections which create sharp contrasts of light and dark might well, when "seen from a distance, live as decoration through the harmony of volumes, planes, and lines."

When Duchamp-Villon enlisted in the army shortly after the outbreak of war in August 1914 he had already made notable progress on what was to be his greatest work. Earlier that year, if not late in 1913, he had modeled a small *Horse and Rider* (fig. 61) in which both figures were treated as semi-mechanical elements, the rider's arms and limbs as rectangular shafts, the muscular structure of the horse's forelegs partially transformed into pistons and wheels. Soon afterwards, in the *Small Horse* (fig. 62), he removed the rider and visualized the body as the opposition of a series of semi-geometrical masses so abstract that the animal's physical characteristics almost disappeared. The next step was still more drastic. The *Head of a Horse* (fig. 63) consists entirely of pseudo-mechanical parts whose arrangement depends more on the sculptural logic of the design than on their resemblance to a horse's head or skull.

This rapid and, as we can now see, daring transmutation of one of the oldest images of human achievement—the equestrian monument symbolizing man's mastery over brute creation and the assertion of his innate intellectual and spiritual dominance—reached its fulfillment in the *Horse* of 1914. Duchamp-Villon died before the final version could be cast.

With every profoundly significant work of art, form and content are not only inseparable, to the degree that any distinction between them can be only a verbal artifice, but each mutually supports the other. The most startling aspect of the *Horse*, to those who first saw it, was its form, its mechanistic appearance. When Matisse visited the sculptor's studio in the fall of 1914 he exclaimed that it was a projectile, "a bomb." The likeness would have been apt, in that first year of the war, and reminds us that Léger was so struck by the glistening beauty of the barrels of the great guns that he began to study the artistic properties of machine-made shapes. But the *Horse* is not the first, even if it remains the most monumental, instance of a machine aesthetic in modern sculpture. Jacob Epstein had already created an image of "the armed sinister figure of today and tomorrow" in his awesome *Rock Drill* of 1912–13 where a seemingly subhuman creature has variously become mechanical. But Epstein's message was particular and exclusive. It said that this was what we might become. Duchamp-Villon's *Horse* is a more general, one would like to say a more metaphysical, statement. "The power of the machine," he wrote Walter Pach, "is upon us, and we no longer can conceive of human beings without it."

From his writings we know that Duchamp-Villon accepted his own times. He was not afraid of the impersonal forces of the industrial age but looked forward to "the point where one views life in such a way that it no longer appears except in the form of a higher dynamics." We may take this higher and inevitably abstract dynamics as the meaning as well as the subject of the *Horse*. Nature has not, as with Epstein, been destroyed in some horrible Frankensteinian nightmare. On the contrary, the physical action of a horse, man's oldest source of energy greater than his own, can be seen and understood as an equation of forces having a tensile strength and beauty peculiar to itself, yet like other sources of ordered power in the industrial world. If we still fear this *Horse*, it may be because the world has turned fearful since Duchamp-Villon first conceived it, for he himself could have had little inkling of the dark way we have had to come since August 1914.

The conception of embodying the power and beauty of the dynamic modern world in artistic form was not Duchamp-Villon's alone. The Italian Futurists had argued and worked for it since 1909. Umberto Boccioni had visited Paris in 1912 and had met Duchamp-Villon, if only briefly. And there are clearly points of contact between French and Italian art in these very years, especially between Marcel Duchamp's *Nude Descend-*

ing a Staircase of 1912 and the first Futurist representations of force in motion through the repetition of identical forms. Nevertheless, Duchamp-Villon's *Horse* has no peer except the very finest of Boccioni's sculptures, and if we prefer it even to the *Unique Forms of Continuity in Space* it must be because of its exceptional concentration of form and content in an image of convincing if inexplicable power.

For the sculptor himself there was little time left. His last work, modeled in 1918, was the *Portrait of Professor Gosset* (figs. 73, 74), one of the physicians who cared for him during his prolonged illness. In this he did to the man's head what he had done earlier to the horse's, reducing it to the least number of shapes, here even fewer, but now less mechanical than organic. To the prosaic mind the portrait may be a severe simplification of Dr. Gosset wearing a hygienic face mask as he makes his hospital rounds. The imaginative critic will see in it overtones of psychic experiences which suggest that, had he been allowed to live, Duchamp-Villon, like his brothers, would have continued to contribute to the development of art in modern times.

George Heard Hamilton

Notes on the Sculptures

My study of Duchamp-Villon began at Yale University under George Heard Hamilton and Robert L. Herbert. It would scarcely be possible to acknowledge in full the ways in which their thinking has affected my ideas. However, I would like to express my gratitude to them for their continuing guidance and encouragement.

Marcel Duchamp extended not only his special knowledge but a courtesy and patience as well which went far beyond matters of family honor, and to him I owe a very special debt.

I would like to thank Alexander Liberman for providing photographs of the Villon studio which enabled me to identify previously unknown works.

I am especially grateful to Edward Fry for his unlimited generosity in making available documents, otherwise inaccessible to me, which allowed me to fill in certain areas of my knowledge. These documents were gathered during the preparation of his book, Cubism, *which, by virtue of a compilation of rare documents and a brilliant analysis, is destined to become one of the standard works on the movement.*

Finally, to my wife, Elita Taylor Agee, my gratitude for many patient and wise suggestions in preparing the notes.

William C. Agee

These notes attempt to publish for the first time the pertinent documents, biography and visual evidence relevant to a sculptor not yet fully appreciated. They are not presented as a catalogue raisonné, for it is by no means certain that other sculptures will not come to light in the near future. However, the full range of Duchamp-Villon's oeuvre, as it is known today, is included. It is hoped that this presentation will establish not only a critical and historical framework for the work of one man, but will in addition suggest some of the most important ideas bearing on modern sculpture in the years from 1900 to 1914.

At certain points it will be noted that the authors diverge in their interpretations of aspects of Duchamp-Villon's art. Since these matters represent issues which are far from closed, no attempt has been made to reconcile them.

Under each note, major group and retrospective exhibitions through 1942 are listed. These exhibitions, which illuminate questions of dating, include the most important showings of Duchamp-Villon's sculpture and list works now lost. A list of exhibitions, including those since 1942, is given in the appendix. Each entry is listed in full as it appeared in the original catalog with known errors retained and so noted. Dimensions are given in inches, height preceding width.

1. **Tête de femme au cheveux longs (Head of Woman with Long Hair)**
c. 1900. Bronze (unique cast). 5½ in. wide
Collection Dr. Robert Jullien, Paris

Although its date is uncertain, this small piece is probably Duchamp-Villon's first extant work. The subject is unknown and the title given here is only descriptive. The vaguely defined figure lying on a flat surface suggests a date as early as 1898–99. At that time Duchamp-Villon was recuperating from a severe illness and, unable to work in a more robust manner, had not yet decided upon a career as a sculptor. The decorative and swirling Art Nouveau lines are the rudimentary efforts of a self-taught artist. He was tentatively exploring the then prevailing idiom with an unsure grasp of his medium and a sensibility still in its formative stages.

2. **Yvette Guilbert**
c. 1901–02. Bronze (unique cast). 5 in. high
Collection Dr. Robert Jullien, Paris

On the basis of its small size and decided Art Nouveau decorative character, this portrayal of the famous Parisian chanteuse may also date a year or two earlier. Although rather cursory and over-stylized, the modeling is more formal, decisive and better controlled. Sweeping lines and broken, impressionist surfaces, modulated to catch the effects of light, place it in the pictorial tradition of such nineteenth-century painter-sculptors as Degas, Renoir and Daumier. The work alludes to the world of urban entertainment and the fashionable café-concert recorded by Manet, Degas, Toulouse-Lautrec, Seurat and the early Picasso.

Yvette Guilbert was one of the most luminous figures of that world. She was painted by Toulouse-Lautrec and Degas and was the subject of a portrait bust done by Medardo Rosso in 1894 (Museo d'Arte Moderna, Venice). Duchamp-Villon chose the moment of her bow in the footlights, which provided an opportunity to blend and dissolve her flowing gown with the stage setting. This impressionist merging of textures, space and solid materials recalls certain works of Rosso, who had achieved some note during his second stay in Paris from 1889 to 1897, and of whom Duchamp-Villon may well have been aware. This assimilation of current painterly modes was both necessary and inevitable for a self-taught sculptor at an early point in his career. Although he was soon to react against this mode, this work marks his full commitment to his art.

Fig. 7   *Head of Woman with Long Hair.*
Bronze, 5½ in. wide. Collection Dr. Robert
Jullien

Fig. 8   *Yvette Guilbert.* c. 1901–02.
Bronze, 5 in. high. Collection
Dr. Robert Jullien

Fig. 9 *Portrait of M. Duchamp.* 1904. Bronze, 14½ in. high. Collection Dr. Robert Jullien

28

3. **Portrait of M. Duchamp**
    1904. Bronze. 14½ in. high
    Collection Dr. Robert Jullien, Paris
    Exh.: 1905, Salon d'Automne

By 1904, after four years of considered and independent study,[1] Duchamp-Villon had attained a sure technical control and was ready to confront the most demanding issues facing sculpture at that time. The most pressing problem was the formidable influence of Rodin, who had rescued sculpture from the abyss of nineteenth-century Salon cupidity and irrelevance and had restored it to a vital and living art. Rodin's technical and expressive innovations held out a new vision for sculpture, extended its means and thereby inexorably altered its course. To absorb and work through the true import of his lessons without falling into an easy parody of his style was a problem facing every serious younger sculptor.

In this portrait of his father, Duchamp-Villon shows mastery and understanding of Rodin's methods. Luminous modeling, through Rodin's "lump and hollow," retains accidental and momentary effects intended to heighten the expressive presence of the sculpture. More important, Duchamp-Villon learned from Rodin's example the necessity of probing the interior, psychological qualities of the sitter, and while the portrait is a Rodinesque exercise, we can discern subtle and individual powers of observation. Duchamp-Villon recorded an image of the rather stiff, self-assured French professional of the middle class with a gentle wit and incisive characterization which forecast the memorable portraits of *Baudelaire* and *Maggy*.

1. Jacques Villon later said of his brother: "Pendant longtemps, il avait compris les choses de l'art en spectateur, de l'extérieur, et même lorsqu'il commença à faire de la sculpture, lorsqu'il entra dans la mêlée, il avait gardé toute son intransigeance d'une personne en somme qui a choisi un certain art." Dora Vallier, *Jacques Villon*, Paris, 1957, pp. 50–51.

4.   Monsieur Prudhomme
       1904. Terra-cotta. 7⅛ in. high
       Collection Jacques Bon, Paris

This caricature was made in an edition of twelve as a prize for a costume dance held at the Bal Tabarin, a popular dance hall in Montmartre. The theme of the dance was based on the characters of Henri Monnier, the well-known nineteenth-century cartoonist. Monsieur Prudhomme, a bourgeois figure of ridicule, was one of the most prominent characters of Monnier's cartoons. Jacques Villon did an engraving in the shape of a fan for the same dance. The wit and caricature are worthy of Daumier, and, although a minor piece, it reveals something of Duchamp-Villon's working methods at that time.

5.   Aesop
       1906. Wax study. 5 in. high
       Collection Jacques Bon, Paris
       Original plaster. c. 6 ft. high
       Present whereabouts unknown
       Exh.: 1906, Salon d'Automne; 1929, Brummer Gallery

It is evident in this work that Duchamp-Villon attempted to move beyond the obvious surface traits of Rodin's style to other less literal aspects of his innovations. Surface detail is suppressed to some degree in favor of larger and bulkier forms. The summary, half-length figure of *Aesop* derives from Rodin's introduction, after 1900, of the fragmented torso, a device which allowed a more compressed and distilled expressiveness and influenced younger sculptors such as Lehmbruck, Brancusi, Maillol, Archipenko and Lipchitz as well as Duchamp-Villon. Furthermore, the shrouded and massive body, enveloped by a pervasive mystery, resembles in both mood and treatment Rodin's controversial *Balzac* (The Museum of Modern Art, New York) of 1897, a work which had created an entirely new emotive range for sculpture. It is also worth noting that the languid, romantic tone of *Aesop* contains remnants of a fin de siècle ennui which is reflected in the titles of missing works of this time, such as *Semper Eadem*, 1904, *Silence* and *Sleep*, both of 1906. The implied mood of faint despair and nostalgia parallels the youthful introspection of Brancusi and Picasso at this time.

Fig. 10 *Monsieur Prudhomme*. 1904. Terra-cotta,
7⅛ in. high. Collection Jacques Bon

Fig. 11 *Aesop*. 1906. Wax study, 3 in. high.
Collection Jacques Bon

31

Fig. 12 *Portrait of Emile Nicolle.* c. 1906. Plaster, 14½ in. high. Collection Madame Duvernoy

6. **Portrait of Emile Nicolle**
c. 1906. Plaster. 14½ in. high
Collection Madame Duvernoy, Paris

Emile-Frédéric Nicolle (1830–1894), Duchamp-Villon's maternal grandfather, was an accomplished engraver who had achieved a certain note with his series of the "Hundred Towers of Rouen." Although Duchamp-Villon did not do much drawing or other art work as a young man, he undoubtedly received his first training from his grandfather, as well as encouragement from his example, when he embarked on a career as a sculptor.

The exact date of the sculpture is not certain, but 1906 seems likely since stylistically it falls between the 1904 portrait of his father and the 1907 *Old Peasant*. Duchamp-Villon probably worked from photographs of his grandfather, as he did later with the portrait of *Baudelaire*. There is considerably less emphasis on the nuances of surface breaks and greater concentration on more incisive cutting of facial characteristics to convey the immediacy of Duchamp-Villon's feeling for the sitter. In this sense it offers a sharp psychological contrast with the more detached and remote image of his father.

7.   **Torse (Torso)**
        1907. Bronze (unique cast). 51¼ in. high
        Musée National d'Art Moderne, Paris
        Exh.: 1907, Salon d'Automne (plaster); 1929, Brummer Gallery

        Study for Torso
        1907. Bronze. 20½ in. high
        Musée National d'Art Moderne, Paris

For Duchamp-Villon 1907 was an important and eventful year. He settled at 7 rue Lemaître, Puteaux, where he worked for the rest of his life, his studio adjoining those of Villon and Kupka. That same year he was appointed to the sculpture jury of the Salon d'Automne, an indication of the respect he had already gained. In addition, he received his first critical notice, in a review of the Salon d'Automne by René Chavance, who commented: "It is here that we find the best sculptures of the entire young school with a torso filled with life and a bust [*Old Peasant*] by Duchamp-Villon."[1]

In the light of these events, *Torso* can be taken as a summation of his career to this point. It demonstrates an accomplished technical command of the sculptor's resources and an ability to employ them with full virtuosity. The modeling represents an extreme of Rodinesque surface agitation, set in motion by the force of light, and tightly compressed within the torso, which is the most direct reflection of Rodin's use of the truncated figure. It is as if Duchamp-Villon had deliberately pushed the lessons of Rodin to an extreme in order to clarify their effective range within his sensibility. Having determined these limits, Duchamp-Villon hereafter sought a very different foundation for his art.

The scientific observation of musculature in *Torso* is the first evidence of the letter-by-letter knowledge of anatomy Duchamp-Villon had acquired as a medical student. All French artists trained at the École des Beaux-Arts were required to study anatomy, but for most it was an academic exercise discarded soon after leaving the École. Many carried out an *écorché*, or flayed anatomical man, as an examination piece. The best known *écorchés* are those by Houdon, Gauguin and Brancusi, but they stand only as curiosities within their oeuvre. Duchamp-Villon himself did an *écorché*, and *Torso* appears as a literal application of its principles. Unlike most artists, Duchamp-Villon retained and extended the implications of anatomy, not only as a means to heightened realism or verisimilitude, but as an intrinsic function of the analysis of structure and movement. As he later impressed upon a student, anatomy was an essential base for building unique and individual forms.[2] However literal the anatomy of *Torso* may be it is the framework that carries the figure and conveys the stress and tension of a potential movement. The figure is caught in an awkward shift between the completed and the anticipated action, rather like a Degas dancer. The coiled pose of the figure is the first example of Duchamp-Villon's lifelong fascination with movement. Movement and anatomy now become a

Fig. 14   *Torso*. 1907. Bronze, 51 ¼ in. high.
Musée National d'Art Moderne, Paris

Fig. 13   *Study for Torso*. 1907. Bronze, 20½ in. high.
                Musée National d'Art Moderne, Paris

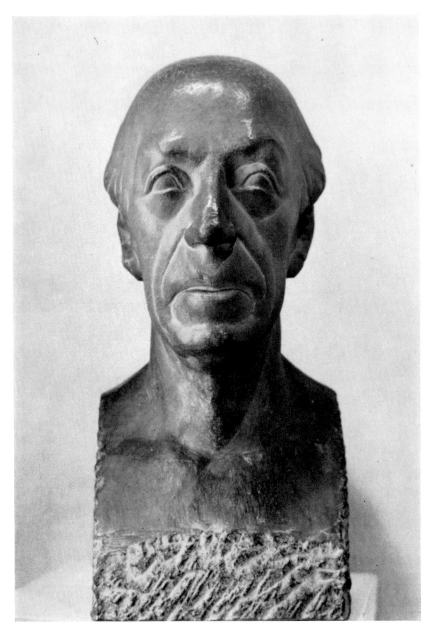

Fig. 15   *Old Peasant*. 1907. Terra-cotta, 20½ in. high. Collection Madame Duvernoy

36

means of learning, for, as he later observed, "an artist's constant concern is to know one object or several."[3]

In progressing from the study to the finished version of *Torso* Duchamp-Villon established the basis of the working process he would employ in most of his later sculpture. The study embodies the broad outlines and essential ideas contained in the artist's initial conception, and is frequently rough and tentative in comparison to the final state from which extraneous details were eliminated.

1. Quoted in *Sculptures de Duchamp-Villon*, Exhibition catalog, Galerie Pierre, Paris, 1931. Exact date and source unknown.

2. "Stories and Anecdotes about Some Early Cubists," unpublished memoir of Mrs. André Roosevelt, now in possession of Mrs. William Wesley, New York. Mrs. Roosevelt had gone to Paris in 1910, and studied with Duchamp-Villon for about two years. She exhibited at the 1912 Salon d'Automne before returning to the United States.

3. "Variations de la connaissance pendant le travail d'art," unfinished manuscript found among Duchamp-Villon's papers. Published in Walter Pach, *Raymond Duchamp-Villon*, Paris, 1924, pp. 27–34. Hereafter referred to as "Variations."

8.   **Vieux Paysan (Old Peasant)**
       1907. Terra-cotta. 20½ in. high
       Collection Madame Duvernoy, Paris
       Exh.: 1907, Salon d'Automne

       Stone. Dimensions unknown
       Estate of the Artist
       Exh.: 1909, Salon d'Automne; 1914, Galerie André Groult; 1929, Brummer Gallery

This portrait, which was exhibited with the *Torso* at the 1907 Salon d'Automne, was completed while Duchamp-Villon was on vacation, probably early that summer, at his in-laws' home at Moret-sur-Loing. The sitter, possessed of a memorable face, was Père Bergeron dit Champonaire, an old and long-time resident of the town.

It was probably executed immediately after *Torso*, and as such is part of that transitional moment in Duchamp-Villon's career when he began to move away from the pervasive influence of Rodin. Surface incident is sharply reduced, with a new emphasis on broad and deep cutting of the facial details, and the effects of light are gauged by large planes rather than infinite breaks. It is apparent that Duchamp-Villon is seeking here a less elusive structure, and to this end he stabilizes the portrait along a frontal and symmetrical axis. His need for greater structural solidity was expressed when he translated the portrait into stone the next year.

9.   Yvonne

1908. Bronze. 10⅝ in. high
Collection Madame Duvernoy, Paris
Exh.: 1919, Salon d'Automne; 1951, Galerie Pierre

Terra-cotta study. 8½ in. high
Collection Dr. Robert Jullien, Paris
Exh.: 1951, Galerie Pierre

Plaster study, same dimensions
Collection Albright-Knox Art Gallery, Buffalo
Exh.: 1929, Brummer Gallery

The conception of the portrait of his sister Yvonne, then twelve years old, in two distinct stages is an explicit rejection of the impressionist image of momentary sensation. The first version relates to the second not as a conventional preliminary sketch but as a less developed state in the formal evolution of a materialized idea. The first stage summarizes the sitter's characteristics through broad and rounded planes rather than by means of surface manipulation. In the final version, all vestiges of the immediate and particular expression are removed, the head is made more ideal, and is stabilized by the cylindrical, shaftlike neck. To further remove the portrait from the momentary, Duchamp-Villon added the exotic chignon, giving the romantic aura of a Gauguin mask. Duchamp-Villon had undoubtedly seen the large Gauguin retrospective at the 1906 Salon d'Automne and would have been impressed, if only briefly, by the hieratic qualities of Gauguin's carved heads. These same heads influenced, to some extent, the primitive masks in Picasso's *Demoiselles d'Avignon* of 1906–07 (Museum of Modern Art, New York).

Duchamp-Villon's method had clearly shifted to a selective process determined by a conceptual apprehension of visible reality. Earlier indications of disaffection with the impressionist surface of myriad dissolving planes culminated in 1908 with his rejection of the premises of an art based on pure sensation. The last stages of the nineteenth-century painterly tradition embodied by Rodin had become exhausted, overworked and, most important, structurally incomplete. This rejection of intuitive sensation coincides with a general and crucial shift of emphasis marking the beginning of early twentieth-century art. The pivotal moments in this shift were the Cézanne retrospectives at the Salon d'Automne from 1905–07, which revealed a lucid system of pictorial structure, the early Cubist explorations of Picasso and Braque in 1908, and Brancusi's carved heads and figures of 1908–09 which also embodied a rejection of Rodin for a formal reductive process. In this sense, the beginning of Duchamp-Villon's modernity appears at an earlier point than has been supposed.

Fig. 16   *Yvonne.* 1908. Terra-cotta, 8 in. high.
Collection Dr. Robert Jullien

Fig. 17   *Yvonne.* 1908. Bronze, 10⅝ in. high.
Collection Madame Duvernoy

10.   Chanson (Song)

1908. Plaster. Dimensions unknown
Present whereabouts unknown
Exh.: 1908, Salon d'Automne

1909. Wood. 21 in. high×38 in. wide
The Art Institute of Chicago, gift of The Arts Club of Chicago
Exh.: 1909, Salon d'Automne; 1914, Galerie André Groult; 1919, Salon
d'Automne; 1926, Salon des Indépendants; 1929, Brummer Gallery

Although Duchamp-Villon had turned from Rodin's stylistic premises, the great
example of Rodin's vitality and force always served him as a point of departure. *Song* is
his first attempt to fuse the sensual with the intellectual, as well as the natural with the
synthetic. It was a process in which he insisted on a fundamental study and knowledge
of natural sources as the basis for a theoretical arrangement of formal elements.

The process began with his ingrained knowledge of anatomy, and was expanded
by drawing from the model, who made weekly visits to the studio at this time and
thereafter until 1912. In *Song* his anatomical knowledge is transformed from specific
details into a schematic and condensed representation in which the long clusters of

muscles, begun in the striations of the arms and legs, form the primary structural frame-work in the manner of the *écorché*. Two drawings which relate to *Song* demonstrate the progressive accumulation of observed natural fact. The first (fig. 19) is a relatively informal outline of the extension of limbs in motion.[1] The second (fig. 20) is more finished, and is rendered in strong contrasts which are as much an analysis of sculptural density as of light and shadow.

Movement, felt only as a potential in *Torso*, becomes real and complex in *Song*. From the evidence of the drawings, Duchamp-Villon, like Rodin, allowed the models to wander freely in the studio, observing them in various attitudes, until they assumed the particular position he wanted. To check his observation and pursue his fascination with movement, he consulted a scientific record of sequential motion. In 1901, Eadweard Muybridge published *The Human Figure in Motion*, in which photographic sequences of various movements were taken from three angles simultaneously. Muybridge's research attracted the immediate attention of artists as well as scientists, and his work was well-known by the Duchamp brothers.[2] The relationship of the figures in *Song* to sequences in Muybridge of a seated figure slightly turning with arm raised makes it clear that Duchamp-Villon used Muybridge to confirm his own observation.

The composition of *Song* is determined from the multiplicity of formal alternatives suggested by acute study of the figure. The figures are virtually identical, but reversed, and their touching arms form a pyramid which locks the composition and creates a contained, geometrically bounded space. Within the outlines thus defined, lines of force run through the figures creating a balance and counterbalance of the statics of motion. Although the figures are rather awkward, a harmony between motion and equilibrium nevertheless emerges.

1. None of Duchamp-Villon's drawings are dated, but on visual evidence most appear to have been done between 1908 and 1912 with the exception of those so noted.

2. Reported to the author by Marcel Duchamp.

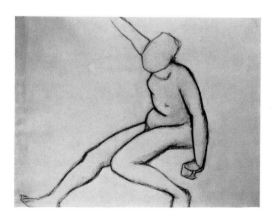

(Opposite) Fig. 18 *Song*. 1908. Wood,
21 in. high × 38 in. wide. The Art Institute
of Chicago, gift of The Arts Club of Chicago

Fig. 19 *Seated Woman*. Charcoal,
20 × 25⅞ in. Musée National d'Art
Moderne, Paris

11.   Jeune fille assise (Seated Girl)

1909. Bronze (unique). 25¼ in. high
Collection Niels Onstad, Los Angeles
Exh.: 1909, Salon d'Automne; 1914, Galerie André Groult (terra-cotta:
location unknown); 1919, Salon d'Automne; 1929, Brummer Gallery
(terra-cotta)

It is apparent from the classic serenity of the expansive and refined volumes found in the seated figure that the sculpture of Aristide Maillol, which stood at an opposite pole from Rodin, had deeply impressed Duchamp-Villon. Whether he knew Maillol cannot be confirmed, but Maillol exhibited regularly at the Salon d'Automne and by 1909 had achieved a considerable reputation. His impressive *Mediterranean* (Museum of Modern Art, New York) shown at the 1905 Salon must be considered a prototype of the *Seated Girl*, both in plastic fullness and in measured, contained space. Maillol later stated that *Mediterranean* was enclosed in a perfect square and *Ile de France* of 1910 (Museum of Modern Art, New York) in an acute triangle.[1] Duchamp-Villon later told his student,

Fig. 20   *Seated Woman*. Pencil and chalk. 19¹⁄₁₆ × 22⁷⁄₁₆ in. Musée National d'Art Moderne, Paris

Fig. 21   *Seated Girl*. 1909.
Bronze, 25¼ in. high.
Collection Niels Onstad

Fig. 22   *Seated Girl*. 1909.
Bronze, 25¼ in. high.
Collection Niels Onstad

Fig. 23 *Seated Girl*. Charcoal, 17⅜ × 10 ⅓⁄₁₆ in. Musée National d'Art Moderne, Paris

Fig. 24 *Seated Girl*. Pencil, 18½ × 20 in. Musée National d'Art Moderne, Paris

Mrs. Roosevelt, that an imaginary circle should enclose a figure so that if it were rolled down a hill nothing would break from it.[2] For both artists theoretical geometry was a means to measured harmony and stability.

The process of sustaining internal movement within a closed pyramid structure, although more rarified in this work, parallels that in *Song*. Two related drawings again chart the progression from the long sinuous lines of the musculature to the dense, blocklike sculptural forms. Scientific fact is combined with the ideal, endowing the momentary with permanence, by a specific connection between Muybridge's sequence of a seated woman, turning in place, with the pose used by Duchamp-Villon.[3] Will and intellect have replaced the vicissitudes of the eye as the creative impulse of Duchamp-Villon's working process.

1. Andrew C. Ritchie, *Aristide Maillol*, Albright Art Gallery, Buffalo, 1945.
2. Roosevelt, *op.cit.*
3. Muybridge, *op.cit.*, p. 153.

44

12. Pastorale

1910. Plaster. 57⅛ in. high
Musée National d'Art Moderne, Paris
Exh.: 1910, Salon d'Automne; 1919, Salon d'Automne (fragment); 1929,
Brummer Gallery

In a family noted for its rigorous intellectual powers, Duchamp-Villon possessed an inquisitive and speculative mind. He was studious, well-read and passionately interested in the issues revolving around art. He was articulate and logical, a forceful presence among his peers. He had an acute sense of history and of the continuity of the great periods of art, and was thus aware of his own generation's place in the history of art.

His reaction against Rodin and the Impressionists was in great part due to his realization that the tradition of the nineteenth century had deprived sculpture of its once heroic grandeur and preeminence among the arts. The essentially pictorial nature of sculpture in 1900 was the result of its dependence on the innovations of painting. As a consequence, in Duchamp-Villon's estimation, it had become structurally weak. From this time in 1910, he undertook through his work and his proclaimed goals, to reassert for sculpture the autonomy and robust power it had traditionally enjoyed.

Duchamp-Villon argued the necessity of removing sculpture from the realm of modeled "bibelots,"[1] and in 1912 he stated that "the true goal of sculpture is above all architectural."[2] In the context of his work this refers not only to architectonic forms, but to the traditional identity of monumental sculpture with great architectural programs. With predictable logic Duchamp-Villon turned to the source most fully embodying these aims, the art of Greece. It became a major concern for him to find a viable basis for a modern art in the principles that animated the classical tradition, although they had fallen into disrepute through a hundred years of abuse in official Salon sculpture. Rodin sought, in his way, much the same goal, and his example, if not his means, served Duchamp-Villon as impetus to secure for the twentieth century a continuity of tradition.

The ambience of the classical world was first invoked in *Seated Girl* through its mood and pyramidal construction. In *Pastorale*, classical references became more specific and programmatic. The very title of the work, and its allusions to Adam and Eve, imply a golden age and return to a beginning symbolized by the art of Greece. The male–female duality represents the most basic possible image, with a minimum of associative connotations. The image is concentrated on the most direct and purely sculptural realization of plastic qualities, devoid of superfluous elements of expression and modeling. The formal and emotive austerity of *Pastorale* reveals Duchamp-Villon's interest in the classic to be focused on the directness of archaic sculpture of the sixth and early fifth centuries, rather than the elaborate manner of Praxiteles of the fourth century.

The traditional identity accorded to sculpture in its relation to architecture is asserted by Duchamp-Villon in placing the two figures within the format of a capital.

Fig. 25 *Pastorale*. 1910.
Plaster, 57⅛ in. high. Musée
National d'Art Moderne, Paris

While the capital bears some similarity to the Romanesque, more likely it was conceived as a composite structure designed to best define and contain the two figures, whose placement and attitude are determined by the outlines of the structural block. Within the enclosing space the figures are in the classical tradition of order, clarity and autonomy of parts. Perhaps the essence of this tradition, however, is the fusion in the striding figures of a state of action with restrained harmony and equilibrium. This sense of harmony was noted in the most extensive critical review Duchamp-Villon had received to date in an article on the Salon d'Automne by Léon de Saint Valéry.[3]

1. "Réponse à une enquête au sujet de *La Danse* de Carpeaux à l'Opéra," *Gil Blas*, September 17, 1912. Reprinted, p. 113.
2. *Ibid.*
3. Reprinted Galerie Pierre catalog, *op. cit.*

13.   **Torse de jeune homme (Torso of a Young Man)**
1910. Bronze. 21⅝ in. high
Louis Carré, Paris (no base)

Terra-cotta. 22¾ in. high
Private collection, New York

Plaster. 24 in. high
The Joseph H. Hirshhorn Collection

Bronze. 22 in. high.
Collection Mrs. Walter Pach (Nikifora N. Iliopoulos)
Exh.: 1913, Armory Show (plaster); 1914, Mánes Society, Prague; 1914,
Galerie André Groult (terra-cotta); 1926 Salon des Indépendants (terra-
cotta); 1929, Brummer Gallery (terra-cotta); 1931, Galerie Dru Bourgeat
et Van Gelder; 1931, Galerie Pierre (terra-cotta); 1942, Galerie de France

Intrinsic to Duchamp-Villon's exploration of the past was a conscious use of traditional
themes and motifs in a modern context as part of his search for a continuity within the
mainstream of history. In the *Torso of a Young Man* he made specific reference to
archaic Greek sculpture through the broad, distilled planes, tightly fitted cap of hair, and
impassive head with single unbroken lines connecting the eyebrow and the nose. The
figure is in fact derived at least in part from the two warriors on the east pediment of
the Temple of Aphaia at Aegina, preserved in the Munich Glyptothek and known to
Duchamp-Villon in reproductions.[1] The figure is condensed, but the energetic thrust of
the striding figure is clearly the same. The values of archaic Greek art—plastic fullness,
strength and directness—correspond to those sought by Duchamp-Villon and others in
the early twentieth century. Maillol traveled to Greece in 1908, and returned deeply
impressed, particularly with the simplicity of archaic sculpture. Archipenko, after coming
to Paris in 1908, also studied archaic sculpture in the Louvre.

The pose of *Torso of a Young Man* which is related to the male figure of *Pastorale*,
has fascinated artists throughout the history of Western art, and in the late nineteenth
and early twentieth centuries it reappeared as part of a classical program which, with the
exception of Cézanne, we have not fully appreciated. Rodin had used the theme in the
Walking Man of 1877 (Collection Edward Steichen, West Redding, Connecticut), a
turning point in modern sculpture. It continues in the path of Cézanne's *Boy Bather*,
c. 1885 (Museum of Modern Art, New York), Maillol's *Blanqui Monument*, c. 1906
(Metropolitan Museum of Art, New York), certain figures of Bourdelle, and Picasso's
classic period of 1905–06, particularly *Boy Leading a Horse*, 1905 (Museum of Modern
Art, New York). For these artists, as well as for Archipenko, Modigliani, and, in a special
sense, Brancusi, the classic tradition represented not a Salon nostalgia or romanticism
for the venerable but a set of working principles held still essential. It was in this spirit

Fig. 26 *Torso of a Young Man*. 1910. Plaster, 24 in. high.
The Joseph H. Hirshhorn Collection

48

Fig. 27 *Torso of a Young Man.* 1910. Bronze, 21⅝ in. high. Collection Louis Carré

that Duchamp-Villon wrote in 1913, "I do not believe that each epoch creates all parts of its aesthetic, but that it finds its roots in the preceding generations which have prepared the way."[2] A child of French rationalism, Duchamp-Villon placed himself in the long line of artists from Poussin, Ingres, Puvis de Chavannes and Seurat who called on the nobility of the past as a viable basis for a modern art.

Traditional methods are recorded as a cumulative process with the *Torso of a Young Man*. The figure was worked from a model, the face derived from a general likeness of his brother Marcel,[3] a measure of his continuing insistence on a close study of sources in nature. The clarity and autonomy of each anatomical component can be traced to the structural patterns of musculature in the *écorché*. In addition, the pose bears a striking relation to the *Gladiator of Agassas*, an *écorché* in common use at the École and reproduced in contemporary books on artistic anatomy,[4] and which may have partially inspired the conception of the figure.

A pyramidal order of construction was evident in the earlier sculpture, *Song* and *Pastorale*. It appears again in the *Torso of a Young Man*,[5] leading to the conclusion that Duchamp-Villon may well have employed a system of proportion derived at least in part from Leonardo's *Treatise on Painting*. The treatise was well-known at Puteaux, and Villon used sections of it in many of his paintings throughout his life.[6] A drawing (fig. 28), based on his *écorché*,[7] and dating from this time, demonstrates the way in which this system was applied first in a sketch before its probable adaption to sculpture. Four triangles converge at an apex which determines the center of balance and the enclosing three-dimensional space of the figure. Another canon, the ancient module based on the head, is also used in a one to seven proportion to arrive at the length of the figure. The theoretical outlines of the drawing also relate to Alberti's method of extending a halo across the top of the head from which lines are dropped to measure the planes that enclose the three-dimensional bulk of the figure. Duchamp-Villon's use of these canons is part of a search for a rational art which became a major concern of the Puteaux Cubists in the years before the war.

The massive planes of *Torso of a Young Man* are related to the sculptural density of Picasso's paintings of 1908 such as *Homme nu assis* (Galerie Percier, Paris). Duchamp-Villon could have seen work of this period at Vollard's Picasso exhibition in 1909. Certainly Duchamp-Villon was well aware of early Cubism for, as he said in 1911, he had been "attracted by the Cubist painters, without knowing them, since the beginning."[8] The relation of Duchamp-Villon's work to Cubism is, as shall be discussed later, always a very special and complex question. It is tempting, but probably premature, to see here the first evidence of a conscious use of early Cubist planes within the context of a traditional figure. These planes may have been tentatively used to accentuate the forms. However, it is most likely that only an analogy exists, at this point, between the goals of early Cubism and those which Duchamp-Villon was seeking through means of archaic Greek sculpture. This in itself, however, was shortly to bear heavily on just those phases

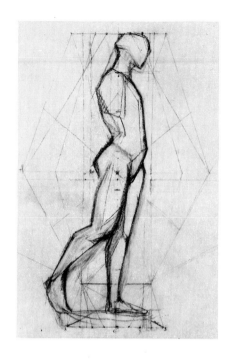

Fig. 28 *Man, Study in Proportion*. Charcoal,
14¾ × 12⅜ in. Musée National d'Art Moderne,
Paris

of Cubism Duchamp-Villon was to explore most fruitfully. In the context of Duchamp-Villon's work, however, it is difficult to distinguish between an analysis based on the *écorché* and the possible influence of Picasso's work of 1908–09. One can best conclude that it was precisely because of this convergence that Duchamp-Villon immediately understood the impact of Cubism. Just how it affected his thinking became clear within the next two years.

1. Walter Pach, *Raymond Duchamp-Villon*, Paris, 1924, p. 16 (hereafter referred to as *Pach*). Pach was a faithful, straightforward reporter of Duchamp-Villon's sculpture; his statements are reliable and confirmed by visual comparison.

2. Letter to Walter Pach, January 16, 1913. Reprinted in *Pach*, p. 17.

3. Reported to the author by Marcel Duchamp.

4. See for example, Mathias Duval and Édouard Cuyer, *Histoire de l'anatomie plastique*, Paris, 1898, p. 253 ff., for extensive description and numerous reproductions of the *écorchés* used at the École.

5. *Pach*, p. 15, reported that Duchamp-Villon "constructed with pyramids." Although the statement was not made with reference to a specific work, it is evidence of the idea within the thinking of the man who knew his work and his means in depth.

6. Reported by Marcel Duchamp; also see Vallier, *op. cit.*, p. 62. See also John Golding, *Cubism: A History and Analysis, 1907–1914*, New York, 1959, p. 168. Villon's interest in geometric ratios led him to suggest the name for the 1912 Section d'Or exhibition at the Galerie La Boétie.

7. See Alexander Liberman, *The Artist In His Studio*, New York, 1960, No. 94, for photographs of the Villon studio in which was preserved the *écorché*.

8. Manuscript notes, Part III, reprinted, p. 111.

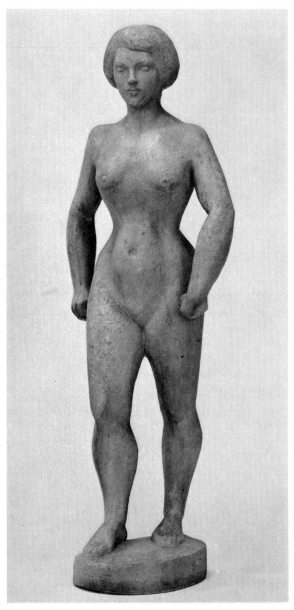

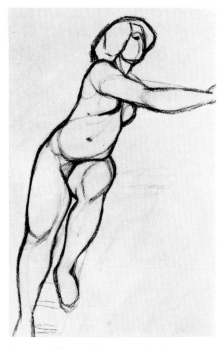

Fig. 29 *Girl of the Woods.* 1911. Terra-cotta, 30¼ in.
high. Collection The Solomon R. Guggenheim Museum,
New York

Fig. 30 *Woman Seated on a Stool.*
Charcoal, 20 × 13 in. Musée National
d'Art Moderne, Paris

14.	**Fille de bois (Girl of the Woods)**
1911. Terra-cotta. 30¼ in. high
Collection The Solomon R. Guggenheim Museum, New York
Exh.: 1911, Salon d'Automne (bronze: whereabouts unknown); 1913,
Armory Show (bronze); 1919, Salon d'Automne (terra-cotta); 1929,
Brummer Gallery (terra-cotta)

This work seems to be a momentary relaxation of Duchamp-Villon's energies, and is his last reference to archaic Greek sculpture. The figure is in the rigid stance of the Greek *kore*, a pose on which Maillol had based his series of the *Four Seasons* of 1910–11, particularly *Flora* of 1911 (Museum of Modern Western Art, Moscow), and which may have inspired Duchamp-Villon.

The sculpture is primarily interesting as evidence of the way the *écorché* continued to function in the analysis of three-dimensional structure. The striations of the hands and feet run through the arms and legs and into the mid-section. They are then pulled together to establish clear zones of component anatomical units. This method is indicated in the drawing (fig. 30) which shows the lengths of connecting muscles running throughout the figure and isolating each section. It is a process which ultimately leads to the elliptical fragmentation of the *Seated Woman* of 1914.

15.	**La vasque décorative (Decorative Basin)**
1911. Stone. 36 in. high. Width 21 in. top
Williams College Museum of Art, Williamstown, Massachusetts
Exh.: 1911, Salon d'Automne; 1912, Salon d'Automne; 1914, Mánes
Society, Prague; 1914, Galerie André Groult; 1919, Salon d'Automne;
1926, Salon des Indépendants; 1929, Brummer Gallery; 1931, Galerie
Dru Bourgeat et Van Gelder; 1931, Galerie Pierre; 1942, Galerie de France

Bronze. 22⅞ in. high
Collection Galerie Louis Carré
Exh.: 1931, Galerie Pierre

Drawings: Musée National d'Art Moderne, Paris

In 1910 a large exhibition of German decorative arts was held at the Salon d'Automne. While the exhibition was perhaps not brilliant, by contrast it did serve to point out the abysmal level of fashionable French decorative arts. Alarmed by the situation, Frantz Jourdain, President of the Salon, appealed to French artists and decorators to renew their efforts in the decorative arts and invited them to exhibit at the Salon d'Automne.[1]

Duchamp-Villon's pride in the French heritage and his nascent concern for the social role of the arts led him to respond to the appeal. He wrote, "the decorative arts have never been so poor in France . . . we live only on a glorious past . . . we must defend our reputation,"[2] and answered the challenge with the *Decorative Basin*, a fountain basin. André Mare, whom he met at this time, may have encouraged him. Mare, a former painter, had by then devoted himself to the decorative arts, and was perhaps inspired by Jourdain's appeal. Their common interest resulted in a small en-

Fig. 31 *Decorative Basin.*
1911. Bronze, 22⅞ in. high.
Collection Louis Carré

Fig. 32 *Decorative Basin.*
1911. Stone, 36 in. high, width
21 in. top. Williams College
Museum of Art, Williamstown,
Massachusetts

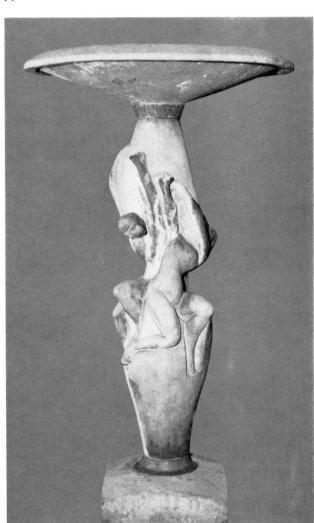

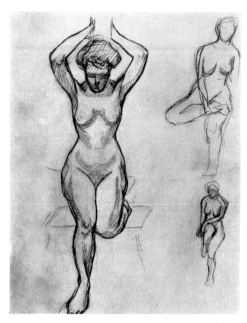

Fig. 33 *Decorative Basin*. Charcoal, 19 × 12 in. Musée National d'Art Moderne, Paris

Fig. 34 *Decorative Basin*. Charcoal, 20 × 13 in. Musée National d'Art Moderne, Paris

semble at the 1911 Salon designed by Mare, to which Duchamp-Villon contributed his portrait of *Baudelaire*.[3] The *Basin* may have been placed near the ensemble. At Mare's invitation, Villon, Léger, La Fresnaye, Laurencin, Rouault and Segonzac also contributed to the ensemble. This was the beginning of a collaboration which was to have important consequences for Duchamp-Villon's art.

Decorative Basin consists of a basin supported by a stand carved in the form of a male and a female figure, an elaborate and baroque variation of *Pastorale*. The figures are conceived architecturally, intertwining through a contrapposto to carry and fill the supporting pedestal. Two drawings, which probably relate to the *Basin*, reveal first (fig. 33), a study from the model, and second (fig. 34), an adaption of this pose to the format of a large fountain.[4] This setting is reminiscent of a seventeenth-century public fountain, a general conception of which may have been the source for the two figures.

1. See Marie Noëlle Pradel, "La maison cubiste en 1912," *Art de France*, I, 1961, p. 178.
2. Manuscript note, reprinted, *Ibid.*
3. *Ibid.*
4. Duchamp-Villon apparently did another version of the *Basin* in 1913 which was exhibited at the Galerie André Groult in 1914 and which was listed as *Vasque décorative pour un jardin* (Decorative Basin for a Garden). The present whereabouts of this piece are unknown, but it may be that this drawing is a study for it.

16.   Baudelaire

1911. Bronze. 15½ in. high
The Joseph H. Hirshhorn Collection, New York
Exh.: 1911, Salon d'Automne; 1911, Galerie de l'Art Ancien et de l'Art
Contemporain; 1913, Armory Show; 1914, Mánes Society, Prague; 1914,
Galerie André Groult; 1919, Salon d'Automne; 1926, Salon des Indé-
pendants; 1931, Galerie Pierre; 1942, Galerie de France

Terra-cotta. 15½ in. high
The Art Gallery of Ontario, Toronto, given in memory of Harold
Murchison Tovell and Ruth Massey Tovell by their sons
Exh.: 1929, Brummer Gallery

Study: Bronze. 3 in.
Collection Jacques Bon, Paris
Exh.: 1931, Galerie Pierre

Drawing: Charcoal. 23¼ × 17⅝ in.
Musée National d'Art Moderne, Paris

By 1911 the revolutionary innovations of Cubism had spread beyond the immediate circle of Picasso and Braque to the group of artists who began meeting regularly that year at Villon's and Duchamp-Villon's studios at Puteaux.[1] The group included the Duchamp brothers, Metzinger, La Fresnaye, Léger, Picabia, Delaunay, Lhote, Kupka and Gleizes. On occasion they were joined by the poets and critics Guillaume Apollinaire, Roger Allard, Alexandre Mercereau, Paul Eluard, André Salmon and Paul Fort. They met on Sundays and later on Monday evenings as well at Gleizes' studio in Courbevoie. All matters of current interest were discussed, including the new art, philosophy, poetry, literature, photography, mathematics and the sciences. Duchamp-Villon was a lively participant, and there can be no doubt of the importance of this forum as an intellectual catalyst for him.

During 1911, as Cubism was assimilated in the work of the Puteaux artists, the group came to view themselves as distinct and separate from Picasso and Braque. Perhaps their most profound difference, apart from their varying formal adaptions of Cubism, was in their outlook on the relation of the new art to the vast changes wrought by modern life. While Picasso and Braque concentrated solely on stylistic problems, those of the rival group, particularly Duchamp-Villon, Gleizes, Metzinger, La Fresnaye and to a lesser extent Villon, attempted to relate Cubism to the epic themes born of the dynamism of a new century.

Amid the emergent social ideals at Puteaux, Duchamp-Villon became intensely conscious of the need for an art appropriate to the twentieth century. His sense of the continuity of history focused on Baudelaire, his spiritual ancestor, who had proclaimed

Fig. 35 *Baudelaire*. 1911. Bronze, 15¾ in. high. Collection, The Museum of Modern Art,
New York. Alexander M. Bing Bequest

the advent of a modern era a half century earlier. In his essays on the Salon of 1846, entitled "On the Heroism of Modern Life" and "The Painter of Modern Life" of 1863, Baudelaire had defined the special qualities of the age and called for an art that would interpret the age to itself on its own unique terms. It is fitting that Duchamp-Villon's first mature work linked him with the poet whose call he was to answer.

Duchamp-Villon worked from photographs of Baudelaire, probably those taken by Nadar and Carjat, which had been given to him by his friend, the literary critic Jacques Crepet.[2] The famous Baudelaire features, the high forehead and thin mouth, were subjected to progressive stages of reduction and redefinition through two preliminary versions. The first resembles Rodin's portrait of Baudelaire of 1898 (Collection Harold Tovish, Brookline, Massachusetts) in the upward gaze and full delineation of facial details. The second is marked by an elimination of these details and the beginning of the exaggerated cranium which characterizes the final version. The two early stages are more than studies or sketches in the conventional sense; rather they are part of the genesis of an idea which materialized through an evolution of conceptual states. This process was first evident in *Yvonne*, and with *Baudelaire* it was established as the working process to be used throughout his career. The distinction is crucial for an understanding of Duchamp-Villon's intellectual approach. He insisted on this process when he later said: "An artist's life is nothing more than a search for perfection. . . . The life of imagination is no more than a series of newly articulated states of consciousness. . . . One could almost say that the sculptor, bit by bit, brings his immaterial creation down to the point where it is crystallized in matter."[3]

As a formal basis of this evolution, Duchamp-Villon readmitted Rodin's method of modeling to his vocabulary. As a mature artist, he could select and transform elements as his own. That Rodin's example was too strong to ever completely ignore is further indicated by the remarkable similarity between the final version of Duchamp-Villon's *Baudelaire* with Rodin's description of his own portrait of the poet. When he was first offered the commission, Rodin flatly refused to do a full-length figure, arguing:

> What is a statue after all?: a body, arms, legs covered with banal clothing. What do these have to do with Baudelaire, who lived only by his brain? With him, the head is every-thing. . . . See the enormous forehead, swollen at the temples, dented, tormented, hand-some nevertheless . . . the eyes have the look of disdain, the mouth is sarcastic, bitter in its sinuous line, but the swelling of the muscles, a little fat, announces his voluptuous appetites.[4]

Duchamp-Villon's portrait is a veritable embodiment of this description, a memorable image revealing his ability to sustain ideas through plastic equivalents without resorting to literary or rhetorical devices. It is another example of his conscious restatement of an existing theme in the light of a modern program.

At Puteaux, the Duchamp brothers spoke of the head in terms of its underlying

Fig. 36 *Study for Baudelaire.* 1911. Bronze, 3 in. high. Collection Jacques Bon

Fig. 37 *Baudelaire.* Charcoal. 20 × 18⅜ in. Musée National d'Art Moderne, Paris

planes. They felt that if it could light up, it would do so according to certain lines of force which represented the object known from its center. These lines defined its form and could be traced and underlined by colored planes.[5] This point affirms *Baudelaire* as the beginning of Duchamp-Villon's radical break with classical modeling-in-the-round. While he had learned to articulate full and robust volumes from archaic Greek art, it was nevertheless the end of a tradition, whose stylistic convention could yield no more to modern goals. Nevertheless, Duchamp-Villon, in a very profound sense, remained within the classical tradition throughout his life. But to reassert its intrinsic principles of clarity, order and autonomy as they had been assimilated by French art, he had to break with its outworn motifs and methods.

Duchamp-Villon looked to the French Gothic as a means of breaking from this tradition. The unity of Gothic sculpture with architecture, as well as its directness within a planar, geometric order, paralleled the ideals Duchamp-Villon sought at this point. Gothic sculpture was still very much within the French artistic consciousness; artists as diverse as Delacroix and Maillol had expressed deep admiration for it, and Rodin had called Chartres the "Acropolis of France." As one of the most glorious chapters in French art, the Gothic appealed to Duchamp-Villon's sense of tradition and his concern for the unity of past with present. He made frequent trips to Chartres, and was well-acquainted with the sculptural programs of the cathedral.[6] *Baudelaire* is remarkably close in spirit and contour to the heads of the Kings of Judah on the right bay of the Portail Royal at Chartres.[7] The quasi-geometric formal reductions of these Gothic heads are more analogous to *Baudelaire* than a possible influence of African art which has been suggested. Although there is some resemblance between the portrait and the masklike, totemic qualities of certain Gabon heads, primitive art was far beyond the restrained French sensibility of Duchamp-Villon. It seems evident that Gothic sculpture provided the example for new expressive possibilities of the human image for Duchamp-Villon in a way equivalent to that provided by African art for Picasso, Braque, Derain and others.

It is probable that Duchamp-Villon turned to the Gothic because it lent itself more readily to and in fact confirmed his increasing experimentation with Cubism. His sober consideration of formal problems meant to some extent that until 1913 he approached Cubism gradually and conservatively. The relation of his work to Cubism in 1911 is thus not easy to establish. We know that he was aware of the Cubists from the beginning, and that he came "little by little to understand their aesthetic and better appreciate it."[8] Certainly his contact with the Puteaux artists hastened his grasp of the tenets of Cubism, but his application of them to sculpture was not clear until 1912. The drawing for *Baudelaire* is more Cubist than the sculpture, and best reveals his approach to Cubism in 1911. It is more geometric in its structure, organized around what Pach termed "the science of planes,"[9] particularly in the closed forms of the eyes, mouth and nose. These geometric shapes correspond to similar elements found in Picasso's work of 1909 such as *Head of a Youth* (Collection Mr. and Mrs. William A. Bernoudy, St. Louis), and especially *Portrait of Manuel Pallares* (Saidenberg Gallery, New York), in which the heads are constructed with angular, sculptural volumes. It is apparent in the drawing that Duchamp-Villon had grasped the significance of Cubism's accentuation, support and essential redefinition of the underlying structural framework. However, the problem to be solved was the way the fundamental reordering of observed reality could be introduced to the solid, physical materials of sculpture. That he applied this conception to the sculpture itself as a reductive process, related to Brancusi's *Sleeping Muse* of 1910 (Art Institute of Chicago), demonstrates something of the special problems raised by Cubist sculpture prior to 1914.

1. See Edward Fry, *Cubism*, New York, 1966, for a chronicle of the development and spread of Cubism in these years; also see Golding, *op. cit.* and Robert Rosenblum, *Cubism and Twentieth Century Art*, New York, 1961.
2. See Marie-Noëlle Pradel, "Nouvelle Acquisitions," *Revue des Arts*: Musées de France, 10, 1960, p. 222.
3. "Variations," reprinted, p. 120.
4. This account was published in 1892; reprinted in Albert Elsen, *Rodin*, New York, 1963, p. 125.
5. Vallier, *op. cit.*, p. 56.
6. Reported to the author by Marcel Duchamp.
7. *Pach*, p. 16.
8. Manuscript note, Part III, reprinted, p. 111.
9. *Pach, op. cit.*

17.   **Maggy**
      1911. Bronze. 29⅛ in. high
      Collection The Solomon R. Guggenheim Museum, New York
      Exh.: 1914, Galerie André Groult; 1925, Galerie Vavin-Raspail; 1929,
      Brummer Gallery (plaster); 1931, Galerie Pierre; 1942, Galerie de France

      Petite Maggy (Small Maggy)
      1911. Bronze. 12¼ in. high
      Collection Mrs. Walter Pach (Nikofora N. Iliopoulos)
      Exh.: 1929, Brummer Gallery; 1925, Galerie Vavin-Raspail

The subject of this portrait was the wife of Georges Ribemont-Dessaignes, a poet and painter who was a frequent visitor to Puteaux. In comparison with her husband she was tall, stocky and rather overbearing. Her features lent themselves to the occasional Duchamp-Villon wit and sense of caricature. *Maggy* is the result of the same method of modification and redefinition established in *Baudelaire*, which provided the source for this stark, massive head set on a cylindrical neck, and it represents a further step away from classical methods of modeling in the round. It is composed of large architectural ridges and hollows organized around a clear-cut vertical axis. The distortions of the head are reminiscent of a medieval gargoyle, and may perhaps derive in part from the Devil's head in the Temptation of Christ on the capital frieze of the Portail Royal at Chartres.

An important precedent was Matisse's *Jeannette* series of c. 1910–11. Duchamp-Villon had probably met Matisse in 1909 when they both served on the committee of the Salon d'Automne. Subsequently they visited each other's studios,[1] and presumably Duchamp-Villon had seen the development of the *Jeannette* head through its five stages. By an evolution similar to Duchamp-Villon's methods, Matisse had moved from the naturalistic phases of I and II to the simplification of III, IV and V (all Museum of Modern Art, New York), the last containing strong affinities with *Maggy*. However, since the exact date of *Jeannette V* is not certain,[2] the possibility of the influence of *Maggy* on Matisse should not be ruled out.

Maggy is the first work of Duchamp-Villon in which an open and definable application of Cubist forms is readily apparent. The high ridges and deep concavities of the head are a realization of the geometric outlines formulated in the Baudelaire drawing, which were not crystallized in the sculpture. That these broad and angular planes are deliberately enlarged and exaggerated is emblematic of Duchamp-Villon's approach to the resolution of the questions raised by Cubist sculpture in 1912. The previous year he had said of sculpture, "Mistress of three dimensions, it has at its service line, plane and volume. The life in its balance, its cadences, its rhythms provides its themes."[3] This statement is at once a reiteration of Cubist principles and an affirmation of an independent sculpture conceived of on its own terms. For it was precisely the lack of these

Fig. 38 *Small Maggy*. 1911. Bronze, 12¼ in. high. Collection Mrs. Walter Pach (Nikifora N. Iliopoulos)

Fig. 39 *Maggy*. 1911. Bronze, 29⅛ in. high. Collection Louis Carré

elements that distinguished our idea of Cubist sculpture up to this time. The two best-known Cubist sculptures, Picasso's 1909 *Head of Woman* (Museum of Modern Art, New York), and Roger de la Fresnaye's *Italian Woman* of 1912 (Galerie Maeght, Paris), were direct translations of paintings: Picasso's *Woman with Pears* of the same year (The Florence May Schoenborn and Samuel Marx Collection, New York) and La Fresnaye's

1911 *Nude* (Philadelphia Museum of Art). The subversion of the autonomy of sculpture, reducing it to its secondary role in the nineteenth century, was intolerable to Duchamp-Villon.

While Cubist painting has been chronicled in detail throughout its complex development, the lack of an adequate history of twentieth-century sculpture has prevented all but the most rudimentary outline of what is even meant by Cubist sculpture. Only the broadest distinction between Analytic and Synthetic has been applied to Cubist sculpture, thus obscuring the crucial stages of its emergence. Early Cubist sculpture has therefore been compared with and judged only on the scale of its painterly complexity relative to Analytic Cubism of 1911–12. However, by the time Cubism had entered this phase—the time at which the movement had become widespread—it was no longer a sculptural style. Early Cubist painting of 1908–09 was composed of closed, geometric forms of substantial bulk organized around relatively stable divisions of the human anatomy. By the end of 1910 the Cubism of Picasso and Braque had changed from its former sculptural conception to an increasingly fragmented, diffuse and painterly mode of open and shifting planes which intersected and merged in a shallow pictorial space. By 1912 this development had brought Analytic Cubism to the antithesis of a sculptural style. Its application to sculpture involved an intrinsic contradiction apparent even in Picasso's *Head of Woman*, which, composed of facet planes, actually indicates a dissolution of the material weight of sculptural form. Duchamp-Villon, faced with this dilemma, looked to the geometric solids of pre-1910 Cubism to create a less elusive and purely sculptural resolution. The head of *Maggy* is thus not an "elementary" application of Cubist forms but rather a logical adherence to the principles embodied in another phase of Cubist art.

If a more searching consideration of Cubist sculpture is extended beyond the confines of 1911–12, it may be that our entire conception of the range of Cubist sculpture must be substantially expanded. For example, considered in the light of Cubist principles of 1908–10, Brancusi's work of these years,[4] especially *The Kiss* (Philadelphia Museum of Art), may be taken as the beginning of a truly independent Cubist sculpture. In addition, the work of Alexander Archipenko, generally considered as Cubist only with the appearance of the 1912 *Walking Woman* (Collection Donald Karshan, New York) emerges in a Cubist vein as early as the 1910 *Hero* (Mrs. Alexander Archipenko, New York). It is clear that the body of Cubist sculpture was more extensive in 1912 than we have imagined.

1. Reported by Marcel Duchamp.
2. See Alfred H. Barr, Jr., *Matisse: His Art and His Public*, New York, 1951, pp. 140–142.
3. "Projet d'article sur le Salon d'Automne de 1911," reprinted, p. 109.
4. I am indebted to Edward Fry for discussing aspects of Cubist sculpture with me which led to these conclusions.

Fig. 40   "*Maison Cubiste.*" 1912. Plaster maquette. Dimensions and whereabouts unknown

18.   "Maison cubiste"
        1912. Plaster maquette
        Whereabouts unknown
        Exh.: 1912, Salon d'Automne; 1913, Armory Show; 1914, Galerie André
        Groult; 1919, Salon d'Automne; 1931, Galerie Pierre

        Drawing: Whereabouts unknown; reprinted from Guillaume Apollinaire,
        Les Peintres Cubistes, Paris, 1913 (1st edition)

The success of the 1911 ensemble at the Salon d'Automne encouraged André Mare to plan a more ambitious project for the Salon of the following year. Mare asked Duchamp-Villon to design a facade that would unify an interior decorative scheme coordinated by Mare himself. Joining Mare and Duchamp-Villon were La Fresnaye, Villon, and Marie Laurencin, who had all participated in the 1911 project, as well as others who were invited to contribute. In the months preceding the Salon the group met once a week to discuss their plans. At Puteaux, Duchamp-Villon carried out the full-scale facade with the help of his brothers. During the period of preparation, the facade came to be known as the "Maison cubiste."[1]

Due to limitations of space and objections raised by Salon officials, only the first floor of the facade was erected at the Salon. Passing through the entrance the visitor came into an interior furnished and decorated in lavish detail. In the entrance way was an iron railing by Richard Desvallières, wallpaper designed by Mare, and Duchamp-Villon's *Decorative Basin*. One proceeded to a large living room which included furniture by Mare, wallpaper by J. L. Gampert, a door panel in relief by La Fresnaye and decorative objects contributed by Maurice Marinot, Paul Vera and others. The room was complete to the inclusion of an inkwell by André Versan and a tea service painted by Villon. Finally, the walls were hung with paintings by Duchamp, Metzinger, Gleizes, Léger and Marie Laurencin. Several sculptures of Duchamp-Villon were included, although we do not know which they were. From the photographs of the interior, an essentially Art Nouveau conception dominated the ensemble which, despite the detailed planning, failed to advance French decorative arts significantly.

The resemblance of certain aspects of Duchamp-Villon's facade to a traditional Louis XVI chateau style has frequently been observed. As a result, the facade has been thought of as unoriginal, thereby overlooking an important aspect of Duchamp-Villon's art theory. The facade was deliberately based, in part, on a traditional style in order to demonstrate the adaptability of the ornamentation to a wide range of architecture and building programs, either already existing or still to be constructed. His conception was not utopian, but motivated by a very real sense of the need to relate a new architectural order to existing surroundings. Duchamp-Villon felt that architecture served as a frame-

Fig. 41 *"Maison Cubiste."* 1912. Plaster maquette. Dimensions and whereabouts unknown

work for all the arts, permitting their cohesion within a logical grouping, and thereby incorporating them as an integral and practical part of society's daily life.[2]

This concern for the relation of art to life was an essential part of the communal spirit which fostered the "Maison cubiste" and was prevalent among the Puteaux artists. It embodied Tolstoy's ideas on art and society set forth in *What Is Art?* (1889), a work widely discussed at the time. It continued the collective venture of the Abbaye de Créteil founded in 1906 by Gleizes, Mercereau, Henri-Martin Barzun and others to further the unity of the arts. Barzun, by 1912 an established member of the Puteaux group, founded that year the magazine *Poème et Drame* which was dedicated to giving voice to the interaction of all the arts in modern life. Most important, this attitude had a profound effect on Duchamp-Villon's major work, *Horse*, and on the painting of other members of the Puteaux group.

The facade however does have elements of the contemporary Beaux-Arts style, and its main outlines resemble the Théâtre des Champs-Elysées, under construction in 1912, suggesting the facade was more modern in conception than might be supposed. In addition, the facade was reportedly more geometric as originally planned and was then modified to suit the space requirements at the Salon.[3] If so, the facade's resemblance to the symmetry of the Théâtre might be more easily imagined. The architect of the Théâtre was Auguste Perret, the most important pioneer of reinforced concrete, a friend of Duchamp-Villon and frequent visitor to Puteaux. Pach reported that Duchamp-Villon said the "Maison" was suggested in part by the new developments in concrete and steel,[4] and we know that he expressed his admiration for the Théâtre.[5]

The most significant aspect of the "Maison cubiste" was the ornamentation applied by Duchamp-Villon. Parts were suggested by natural phenomena, such as the shapes over the entrance which were based on the patterns of icicles hanging in the garden at Puteaux. The central ornament on the second floor, which consisted of intersecting triangular forms, was an abstract translation of the sun and its rays of energy.[6] The central ornamentation was held together by what he termed the "living line"[7] which

Fig. 42 "*Maison Cubiste.*" 1912.
Plaster maquette. Dimensions and
whereabouts unknown

67

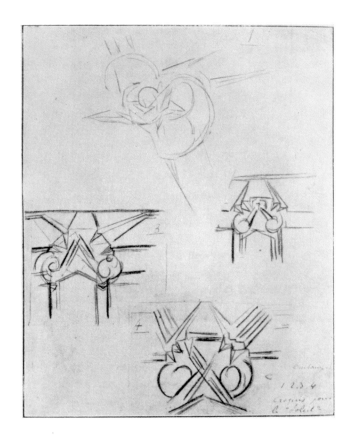

Fig. 43 *"Maison Cubiste."*
1912. Charcoal. Dimensions
and whereabouts unknown

ran through each form and converged at a point directly over the pediment. This point corresponds to what he later described as: "a plumb line, motionless, suspended in the center of a free space. It is the purest element of sculptural language about which man has a certain, indispensable, inexplicable idea. This harmony, absolute and concrete, makes a point of infinity tangible for man."[8]

The precision of the geometric outlines in the ornamentation suggests that Duchamp-Villon may have employed the golden section, the ancient ratio by which a line is divided so that the smaller part is to the larger part as the larger is to the whole. Although it is difficult to determine precise measurements from the photographs, it does appear that Duchamp-Villon employed the mean in the facade. It can be measured in the proportions of the door, the dimensions from the bottom of the door to the top of the windows on the second floor, and in the triangular motifs over the windows and door. The mean served as a method of unifying the overall dimensions with the separate decorative elements.

The system of proportion was discussed extensively at Puteaux as part of the group's search for a more rational, less intuitive basis for their art. Villon realized its importance from reading Leonardo's *Treatise on Painting*, and suggested the title of the famous exhibition of the Salon de la Section d'Or held at the Galerie La Boétie in October 1912, simultaneously with the Salon d'Automne, which was dominated by the Puteaux artists. The golden section was used extensively by Juan Gris, and with less precision by Lhote, Metzinger and Villon, who all took part in the exhibition, to develop and sustain a pictorial structure based on mathematical order.[9]

Duchamp-Villon said of the ornamentation: "It is almost droll the pleasure I have in arranging simple square blocks, the one with the others, until I have found the right relation of forms and dimensions."[10] This statement touches on the implications the "Maison cubiste" had for his sculpture. The arrangement of these geometric shapes, analogous to closed forms of Cubism, permitted him to break completely from a conception of sculpture based on modeling and adhering to a closed, monolithic center. From the "Maison," the basis of his work came to rest on the assembly and construction of purely autonomous shapes. In this sense the ornamentation corresponds to the beginning of collage and synthetic Cubism introduced by Picasso in the spring of 1912. By breaking with the literalness of modeled forms, Duchamp-Villon approached a new range of expressive possibilities, which could fulfill his idea that "We must establish a new decor of architecture, not only in the characteristic lines of our times, which would be but a transposition of these lines and forms in other materials, and which is an error. Rather we must penetrate the relation of these objects among themselves, in order to interpret, in lines, planes and synthetic volumes, which are balanced, in their place, in rhythms analogous to those of the life surrounding us."[11]

1. For a detailed account of the inception of the *Maison*, see Marie Noëlle Pradel, "La maison cubiste en 1912," *Art de France*, I, 1961, pp. 177–186. See also Gustave Kahn, "La réalisation d'un ensemble d'architecture et de décoration," *L'Art décoratif*, February 1913, pp. 89–102.

2. Walter Pach, *A Sculptor's Architecture*, New York, 1913; and *Queer Thing, Painting*, New York, 1938, p. 141; and also *Pach*, p. 13.

3. Pradel, *op. cit.*, p. 182.

4. Pach, *A Sculptor's Architecture*. (No pagination.)

5. Manuscript note. Published Pradel, *op. cit.*, p. 179.

6. Pach, *Queer Thing, Painting*, p. 142.

7. Pach, *A Sculptor's Architecture*.

8. "L'architecture et le fer," *Poème et Drame*, VII (January–March 1914), p. 28. Reprinted, p. 114.

9. See William Camfield, "Juan Gris and the Golden Section," *Art Bulletin*, New York, March 1965, pp. 128–134.

10. *Pach*, p. 14.

11. Letter to Walter Pach, January 16, 1913. Reprinted *Pach*, p. 18.

19.   Les Petits Danseurs (The Small Dancers)
1911–12. Bronze. 6¾ × 17⅜ in.
Louis Carré, Paris

Terra-cotta. 6¾ × 17⅜ in.
Munson-Williams-Proctor Institute, Utica
Exh.: 1913, Armory Show (plaster); 1914, Mánes Society, Prague (terra-cotta); 1914, Galerie André Groult (terra-cotta); 1919, Salon d'Automne; 1925, Galerie Vavin-Raspail (bronze); 1929, Brummer Gallery (plaster); 1931, Galerie Pierre; 1942, Galerie de France

This small relief was probably begun in late 1911.[1] It was originally intended as a study for a larger panel of four or five figures which was to form the central decoration over the entrance to the "Maison cubiste."[2] However, Duchamp-Villon gradually abandoned this idea as the geometric form of ornamentation evolved. Whether that panel or this study was exhibited with the "Maison cubiste" as part of the interior decoration is not known. The relief is the first in a series of architectural panels, comprising a large portion of his work from 1911 to 1913. It reveals his sustained interest in movement first apparent in the 1908 *Song*, and is directly related to a free-standing figure of 1910, *Mouvement de danse* (Estate of the artist). The relief is contained within a shallow pictorial space, in which the figures are condensed forms treated schematically. This space emphasizes the rhythmic lines of flow reminiscent of Matisse's painting *La Danse* of 1910 (Museum of Modern Western Art, Moscow).

1. Dated 1911 by *Pach*, and in catalog of exhibition at Galerie André Groult, April 6–May 3, 1914.
2. Panel now lost; formerly Collection Gabrielle Buffet-Picabia.

Fig. 45   *The Small Dancers.* 1911–12. Bronze, 6¾ × 17⅜ in. Collection Louis Carré

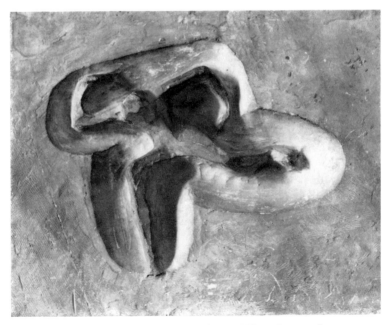

Fig. 44   *Les Petits Danseurs.* 1911–12. Plaster. Whereabouts unknown

71

20. **Le Chat (Cat)**
1913. Concrete. 25½ × 21 in.
Collection The Solomon R. Guggenheim Museum, New York

Wood. 27 × 24⅞ in.
The Detroit Institute of Arts, gift of Robert H. Tannahill
Exh.: 1913, Salon d'Automne; 1914, Mánes Society, Prague (plaster);
1914, Galerie André Groult (wood); 1915, Carroll Galleries, New York;
1919, Salon d'Automne; 1929, Brummer Gallery (plaster); 1931, Galerie
Pierre (bronze)

Le Chien (Dog)
1913. Plaster. Dimensions and whereabouts unknown
Exh.: 1913, Salon d'Automne; 1914, Galerie André Groult (terra-cotta);
1919, Salon d'Automne; 1929, Brummer Gallery (plaster)

Le Perroquet (Parrot)
1913. Wood. 25⅞ × 25¾ in.
Yale University Art Gallery, Collection of the Société Anonyme
Exh.: 1913, Salon d'Automne; 1914, Galerie André Groult (wood);
1927, Anderson Galleries, New York

Les Colombes (Doves)
1913. Concrete. Dimensions and whereabouts unknown
Exh.: 1913, Salon d'Automne; 1919, Salon d'Automne; 1929, Brummer
Gallery

These four reliefs were executed as part of the third and last ensemble planned and co-ordinated by André Mare and shown at the Salon d'Automne of 1913. The ensemble was a small room with furniture and decorative objects designed by Mare, Maurice Marinot, Richard Desvallières and Vallois. On the walls Duchamp-Villon's reliefs were placed next to La Fresnaye's painted panels, the *"instruments jardiniers."*[1] Apparently Duchamp-Villon designed an architectural setting for the ensemble, but no record of it has survived.

The reliefs express Duchamp-Villon's continued concern for the unity of the arts. He said, "If one examines the Egyptian, Greek, Roman and French civilizations, one is struck by the unity which governs their spirit, in their monuments, and in their furniture, costumes and useful objects. One notices only anachronistic and disparate elements in our days."[2]

Fig. 46   *Cat.* 1913. Concrete,
25½ × 21 in. Collection The Solomon
R. Guggenheim Museum, New York

Fig. 47   *Cat.* 1913. Wood, 27 ×
24⅞ in. The Detroit Institute of Arts,
gift of Robert H. Tannahill

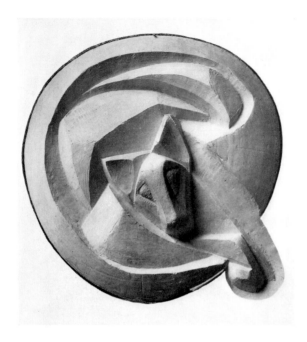

Fig. 48   *Dog.* 1913. Plaster.
Dimensions and whereabouts unknown

Fig. 49   *Parrot.* 1913. Wood,
25⅞ × 25¾ in. Yale University Art
Gallery, Collection of the Société
Anonyme

74

Fig. 50   *The Doves*. 1913.
Concrete. Dimensions and whereabouts unknown

The animal themes were inspired by the menagerie Duchamp-Villon kept at
Puteaux and although the reliefs are his least successful works, they did provide an
important formal lesson. Treated in component sections, they carry his break with
modeling in the round another and decisive step forward. The arrangement of the
sections in an independent structural order extended the implications of the arrangement
of architectural blocks in the ornament of the "Maison cubiste," and continued to
employ Cubism as a means to construct and accentuate volumes, while reflecting a
growing awareness of the more open pictorial systems of Synthetic Cubism.

The shallow space of the reliefs enabled him to experiment with the possibilities of
an overlapping and intersecting network of forms, related to Synthetic Cubism, before
applying them to free-standing sculpture. In addition, the circular format solved the
problem of integrating the animal forms into the full space without encountering awkward corners and edges, a method analogous to the oval format used by Picasso and
Braque after 1910 to resolve similar problems.

1. See *L'Art Décorative*, No. 199 (January 1914). Entire issue devoted to Salon d'Automne of 1913
and the decorative arts. The Mare ensemble with Duchamp-Villon's reliefs are illustrated on p. 54.

2. Letter to Walter Pach, January 16, 1913. Reprinted in *Pach*, p. 18.

21. **Les Amants (The Lovers)**
1913. Bronze. (first sketch) 13½ × 20¼ in.
Private collection, Paris

Bronze. 13½ × 20¼ in.
Louis Carré, Paris

Plaster. 27½ × 46 in.
The Museum of Modern Art, New York

Bronze. (final state) 26¾ × 39⅜ in.
Louis Carré, Paris

Drawing
23½ × 23½ in.
Musée National d'Art Moderne, Paris

Exh.: 1913, Salon d'Automne (final state); 1914, Mánes Society, Prague
(final state, plaster); 1914, Galerie André Groult (terra-cotta and sketch);
1915, Carroll Galleries, New York; 1919, Salon d'Automne; 1926, Salon des
Indépendants; 1929, Brummer Gallery (final state and sketch); 1931,
Galerie Pierre (final state and four preliminary versions); 1942, Galerie
de France

The Lovers culminated the 1913 series of reliefs and, although not part of the Mare
ensemble, it was exhibited that year at the Salon d'Automne. It is by far the most
complex, refined and successful of the series, a measure of the intensive reworking and
revising undertaken by Duchamp-Villon. The theme is one of the many traditional
motifs he drew on in his conscious effort to secure the roots of modern art within the
long heritage of the past. It has references in classical mythology, Renaissance art and
in the erotic themes of Rodin. More specifically, it is directly dependent on Maillol's
1904 relief, *Desire* (Museum of Modern Art, New York). The male and female figures
are reversed, but the main lines of force and the formal accents provide the composi-
tional elements which Duchamp-Villon transformed into a sequence of drastically condensed Cubist incisions.

The process of transformation encompassed four distinct stages prior to the final
version. Some of the intermediate changes are subtle and discrete, but nevertheless
record the perceptible inflections of the, by then, unrelenting formal logic of Duchamp-
Villon. He started with a Rodinesque sketch which indicated the placement of the fragmented and recomposed volumes and the continuous lines binding them within the
spatial frame. The pose of the female figure may have been studied in the drawing from
the model (fig. 55) in which the stresses and turns of kneeling posture were determined.

76

Fig. 51 *The Lovers*. Bronze (first sketch), 13½ × 20¼ in. Private collection, Paris

Fig. 52 *The Lovers*. 1913. Bronze, 13½ × 20¼ in. Collection Louis Carré

78

It was through this drawing that the prismatic shape of the chest evolved, suggesting a lingering dependence on the *écorché* as a basic guide to anatomical and structural divisions which were then given a full geometric autonomy through Cubist accentuations.

The second stage of *The Lovers* (Estate of the artist) tacitly recognized and overcame the cursory and stylized junctions of the animal reliefs by submitting the figures to the limits imposed by a specific architectural format based on a metope or segment of a medieval frieze. The next stages removed the literal confines of this format, but the final composition of the relief was determined by the internal movement and disposition of parts thus accorded. It was this method of definition which prompted Duchamp-Villon to say that the relief had been designed with the logic of a Gothic cathedral.[1] In the final version the anatomical shapes were further refined and reduced to a minimum of working parts. The arrangement of independent forms within the shallow space of the relief extended the lessons of the "Maison Cubiste," by further breaking from the confines of the monolith. It was thus that he could say of the sculpture section at the 1913 Salon d'Automne, "Unfortunately nearly all of it is in the domain of modeling, which is quite far from that of sculpture."[2]

1. *Pach*, p. 12.
2. "Opinions (au Salon d'Automne)," *Montjoie!* v. 1, no. 11–12 (November–December 1913), p. 14.

(Opposite, above) Fig. 53 *The Lovers*. 1913. Plaster, 27½ × 46 in. Collection, The Museum of Modern Art, New York

(Opposite, below) Fig. 54 *The Lovers*. 1913. Bronze (final state), 26¾ × 39⅜ in. Collection Louis Carré

Fig. 55 *Kneeling Woman*. Charcoal, 23½ × 23½ in. Musée National d'Art Moderne, Paris

22.   Projet d'architecture

1914. Plaster maquette. 22 × 13⅜ in.
Collection Mrs. Walter Pach (Nikifora N. Iliopoulos), New York
Never exhibited

In the fall of 1912 Duchamp-Villon met Walter Pach who was in Paris arranging loans for the Armory Show to be held in February 1913. Pach admired his work, and he was primarily responsible for securing Duchamp-Villon's reputation both in Europe and the United States. Pach took several of Duchamp-Villon's sculptures, including the maquette for the "Maison cubiste," for exhibition at the Armory Show. On that occasion he also wrote a small pamphlet, *A Sculptor's Architecture*, which outlined the premises of Duchamp-Villon's architecture. Pach's enthusiasm led a certain Mr. Chappell—we know nothing of him or the institution he represented—to request a plan of sculptural ornamentation for a new dormitory to be built at a college somewhere in Connecticut. In response to the request, Duchamp-Villon designed this maquette and sent it to Pach in New York. Unfortunately the plan was rejected by the college.

Through the same spirit that had prompted the "Maison Cubiste," Duchamp-Villon employed a Gothic style of architecture as the setting to demonstrate that the ornament was suitable for any type of building program.[1] He had consulted reproductions of English Gothic manor houses such as those at Bradfield, Sutton Place and Drakelowe, where a geometric style of decoration predominated and which suggested the series of bas-reliefs incorporated into a wall without interrupting the lines of the building. His style of decoration, he felt, could be adapted to the Gothic without disrupting its inherent unity.[2] There is here an implicit attempt to correlate the methods of Gothic building to a modern structure which continued the efforts of Viollet-le-Duc and later Victor Horta and H. P. Berlage, who had all made extended attempts to apply the principles of Gothic architecture to modern problems and materials.

In the three rows of decoration, Duchamp-Villon established a motif based on the heavens; the upper level represented the planets, the middle level the stars, and the lower level the moon and its rays.[3] Each had an ellipse as a common geometric base on which was introduced a variety of designs, in accordance with principles of alternation which Duchamp-Villon saw as one of the secrets of the Gothic.[4] The orientation of the designs was, like all Cubist art, essentially realistic, for as Duchamp-Villon said, ". . . the pleasure is in finding motifs which have their origin in life, no matter how abstract the realization may appear."[5] The formal elements of these motifs derived to a certain extent from the "Maison cubiste." Some, such as the triangular shapes on the second

Fig. 56 *Projet
d'architecture.* 1914.
Plaster maquette,
22 × 13⅜ in.
Collection Mrs.
Walter Pach (Nikifora
N. Iliopoulos)

level, were applied as a single form isolated from the central ornamentation of the
"Maison cubiste." They enabled him to refine and extend the formal organization of
architectural parts in an increasingly abstract context.

1. Letter to Walter Pach, May 14, 1914. Reprinted in *Pach*, p. 21.
2. Letter to Walter Pach, March 17, 1914. *Ibid.*, p. 19.
3. Letter to Walter Pach, May 14, 1914.
4. Letter to Walter Pach, March 17, 1914.
5. *Ibid.*

Fig. 58 *Seated Woman*. 1914. Bronze, 25¾ in. high.
Yale University Art Gallery. Bequest of Katherine S. Dreier

Fig. 57 *Seated Woman*. Charcoal,
17½ × 9¾ in. Museum of Art, Rhode
Island School of Design

82

23. Femme assise (Seated Woman)
 1914. Bronze. 25¾ in. high
 Yale University Art Gallery. Bequest of Katherine S. Dreier for the
 Collection of the Société Anonyme
 Exh.: 1914, Galerie André Groult (bronze); 1915, Carroll Galleries, New
 York; 1919, Salon d'Automne; 1926, The Art Center, New York; 1926,
 Brooklyn Academy of Arts and Sciences; 1951, Galerie Pierre; 1942,
 Galerie de France

 Drawing. Charcoal. 17½ × 9¾ in. Museum of Art, Rhode Island School of Design

Early in 1914 Duchamp-Villon resumed free-standing sculpture and completed *Seated Woman* by April when it was exhibited at the Galerie André Groult. Here he attempted to transpose the formal premises of the network of autonomous sculptural components developed in the reliefs to an equivalent order in three dimensions. He could not quite make a complete shift within this one work for it is essentially realized through a method of traditional modeling. However, it is evident that Duchamp-Villon was seeking to extend the principles of *The Lovers* with a view to attempting an architectural scaffold of constructed parts. Each section of the anatomy is pared down to its essential structure and treated as a separate and distinct element which is then fitted together, one part to another within the sculptural whole, as in a smoothly joined mechanism. It is in *Seated Woman* that we begin to see combined in his work what Villon termed "the engineer, joined with the architect and sculptor."[1]

The pose is a complex and shifting equilibrium between movement and repose, recalling the tenuous balance of Michelangelo's *Madonna and Child* from San Lorenzo, and continuing Duchamp-Villon's long interest in both real and potential movement.

The figure carries the unmistakable look of the most basic of the artist's tools, the mannequin, still used today in the study of human movement and anatomy. An artist's mannequin is actually a streamlined and flexible *écorché* and its grouping of musculature is obviously the source of the extreme divisions of anatomy within *Seated Woman*. The sections of the mannequin undoubtedly assisted Duchamp-Villon in making the difficult transition from relief to three dimensions, first in arranging the pose, and second in eliminating the need to "compose" or "design" the figure, thereby enabling him to concentrate solely on the assembling of the formal elements.

If the mannequin is a most prosaic artist's aid, Duchamp-Villon transformed it into a sleek image of machine-turned precision: the first embodiment of the impact of the modern urban world in his art. Themes related to the machine and the twentieth century had already appeared in the iconography of the Puteaux artists. By early 1913 Duchamp-Villon had come to an acute awareness of the meaning of the machine to the life of the new century.[2] The distilled and glistening plasticity of machined parts of *Seated Woman* found their counterpart in the cylindrical sections of Léger's "tubist" compositions of this time, such as *L'Escalier* (Kunstmuseum, Basle). Mechanical segments also appeared in Metzinger's *Le Gouter* of 1912 (Philadelphia Museum of Art), and, if more ironic, were at the heart of Marcel Duchamp's revolutionary *Nude Descending the Staircase* of 1911 (Philadelphia Museum of Art). Although they are less specifically related to the machine, Brancusi's general process of reduction and Archipenko's *Gondolier* of 1914 (Collection Donald Karsham, New York) parallel the formal qualities of *Seated Woman*. The clean precision and formality of the figure's definition also serve to remind us of Duchamp-Villon's sustained allegiance to the long tradition of French classical art.

1. Jacques Villon, "Duchamp-Villon," *in* Pierre Francastel, *Les Sculpteurs Célèbres*, Paris, 1954, pp. 306–307.
2. See letter to Walter Pach, January 16, 1913; reprinted in *Pach*, p. 19.

24.   **Jeune fille assise (Seated Girl)**
1914. Plaster. 14 in. high
Collection Mr. Vincent Tovell, Toronto
Exh.: 1931, Galerie Pierre

This small plaster has previously been unknown and unpublished. It is probably the piece exhibited in 1931 at the Galerie Pierre, under the title here assigned, *Jeune fille assise*, dated 1914. The work occupies a crucial position in Duchamp-Villon's oeuvre, for it provides the link between the 1913 reliefs, the *Seated Woman* and *Horse*. The figure realizes the architectural conception of sculpture sought in *Seated Woman*. It is a three-dimensional translation of the female figure in *The Lovers* and its component geometric sections, radically simplified as individual parts erected on a framework binding the sculptural whole. These sections are closed, solid forms in keeping with Duchamp-Villon's insistence on a truly sculptural vocabulary, but are based on an understanding of the new developments of Synthetic and Collage Cubism. Of particular importance is the analogy of the triangular base, which enables the figure to turn within an enclosed space, with the new spatial sequences created by the interlocking and overlapping forms of Cubist painting of 1912–14. The implied junctures of an interwoven space in collage are brought forth into the real and tangible materials of sculpture occupying a non-illusionistic space. This turn along a scaffold of intertwining pyramids solved the most difficult problem which confronted Duchamp-Villon in mastering the internal transformation within the *Horse*.

The realization of an architectural conception of sculpture, now completely removed from the domain of traditional modeling, had profound implications not only for *Horse*, but for the entire course of twentieth-century sculpture. Contemporary criticism, although generally vague when dwelling on sculpture, grasped the distinctive character,

Fig. 59   *Seated Girl*. 1914. Plaster, 14 in. high. Collection Vincent Tovell

if not the full import, of this development. Both Salmon[1] and Apollinaire[2] noted the role architecture had played in freeing Duchamp-Villon from the limits of natural representation. It is this conception that distinguishes *Seated Girl* from other Cubist sculpture which appeared in 1914. By comparison, the first Cubist ventures of Lipchitz such as the 1914 *Sailor with Guitar* (Philadelphia Museum of Art), although composed of broad, synthetic planes, appear as direct translations of painting. The same is true of other sculpture we have thought of as more directly Cubist simply because it corresponded to the more easily translated tenets of Synthetic Cubism, namely the work of Laurens from 1914–17 and Juan Gris' *Figure* of 1917. The close approximation and dependence on painting in these works is disclosed by the uniformly thin, planar and vertical quality of their constituent sections. By contrast, Duchamp-Villon deliberately modified and alternated his forms between conical, ovoid and triangular shapes, all common to a sculptural idiom.

1. André Salmon, *La Jeune Sculpture Française*, Paris, 1919, p. 92. (Although not published until 1919, the book had been written in 1914.) See also Salmon's introduction to Catalogue of the exhibition at the Galerie André Groult, April 6–May 3, 1914.
2. Guillaume Apollinaire, *Les Peintres Cubistes*, Paris, 1913, p. 79.

25. Le Cheval (Horse), 1914.

1. **Cheval et Cavalier (Horse and Rider)** (First state)
1914. Bronze. 9 in. high
Collection Mr. and Mrs. William Rand, New York

2. **Cheval et Cavalier (Horse and Rider)** (Second state)
1914. Bronze. 11⅜ in. high
Collection Mr. and Mrs. M. Riklis, New York

3. **Le Petit Cheval (Small Horse)**
1914. Bronze. 11⅞ in. high
Louis Carré, Paris

4. **Tête de Cheval (Head of a Horse)**
1914. Bronze. 19 in. high
The Joseph H. Hirshhorn Collection, New York

5. **Très Petit Cheval (Very Small Horse)**
1914. Bronze. 3½ in. high
Collection Mr. and Mrs. Raymond Pach, Canton, N.C.

6. **Le Cheval (Horse)**
1914. Plaster. 18 in. high
Collection Mme. Duvernoy, Paris

7. **Le Cheval (Horse)**
1914. Bronze. 15⅜ in. high
Collection Edgar Kaufmann, jr., New York

8. **Le Cheval (Horse)**
1914. Bronze. 40 in. high
The Museum of Modern Art, New York. Van Gogh Purchase Fund

Fig. 60 *Horse and Rider* (First state).
1914. Bronze, 9 in. high. Collection
Mr. and Mrs. William Rand

9. **Le Cheval Majeur (Large Horse)**
   1914. Bronze. 59 in. high
   Louis Carré, Paris
   Exh.: 1925, Galerie Vavin-Raspail. *Le Cheval*; 1926, Salon des Indé-
   pendants. *Le Cheval*; 1929, Brummer Gallery. *Le Cheval, Tête de Cheval*
   (wax and plaster), *Study* (probably *Cheval et Cavalier*); 1931, Galerie
   Pierre. *Le Cheval, Le Cavalier Droit* (*Cheval et Cavalier*, first state);
   Le Cavalier Penché (*Cheval et Cavalier*, second state); *Étude de Cheval*
   (probably *Le Petit Cheval*); *Tête de cheval*; *Étude pour Tête de Cheval*;
   Petit Cheval (probably *Très Petit Cheval*); 1942, Galerie de France.
   Le Cheval

   Drawing. Whereabouts and dimensions unknown. Reproduced Walter
   Pach, *Raymond Duchamp-Villon*, Paris, 1924. p. 11

   Drawing. Whereabouts and dimensions unknown. Reproduced *Cahiers
   d'art*. No. 28, 1953, pl. 2

87

Fig. 61 *Horse and Rider*.
(Second state). 1914.
Bronze, 11⅜ in. high. Collection Mr. and
Mrs. M. Riklis

Fig. 62 *Small Horse*. 1914. Bronze,
11⅞ in. high. Collection Louis Carré

"La puissance de la machine s'impose et nous ne concevons plus guère les vivants sans elle. Nous sommes émus d'une manière étrange par le frôlement rapide des êtres et des choses et nous nous habituons, sans le savoir, à percevoir les forces asservies par eux. De là à prendre une opinion de la vie, telle qu'elle ne nous apparaisse plus que sous sa forme de dynamisme supérieur, il n'y a qu'un pas, vite franchi."

from a letter to Walter Pach, January 16, 1913[1]

After Henry Adams visited the Galerie des Machines at the 1900 Exposition Universelle in Paris, he envisioned the Dynamo as the new and destructive force replacing the Virgin as a symbol of the power behind mankind's most cherished aspirations. His alienation was typical of the nineteenth-century reaction and protest against the inexorable course of the technological revolution. Raymond Duchamp-Villon also visited the exhibition; but, by contrast, he could later view the Galerie des Machines as "a work filled with power and audacity, proclaiming, in a fantastic hall, the glory of steel."[2] Duchamp-Villon's generation, which came to maturity in prewar Paris, embraced the machine and the dynamism of a new age with cheerful and eager optimism. This generation seized the implications of the machine and its impact on modern life to bring forth an aesthetic which was an intrinsic part of the revolution then transforming the entire spectrum of the arts. Duchamp-Villon's statement on "the power of the machine" is perhaps the most penetrating revelation of the extent to which the machine had affected the artist's consciousness. While the machine aesthetic was most pronounced among the artists at Puteaux, it appeared in creations as diverse as Stravinsky's *Sacre du printemps*, Futurist art, and the poetry of Blaise Cendrars and Apollinaire. The most profound and complex embodiment of the transition from the nineteenth to the twentieth century is Duchamp-Villon's *Horse*, symbol of a revolution still in progress.

The *Horse* was begun in the spring of 1914, probably shortly after the exhibition at the Galerie André Groult in April.[3] The final version was apparently under way when war was declared on August 3, and was finished in the fall when Duchamp-Villon returned to Puteaux on leave.[4] The work was enlarged from its original state in 1930–31 and again in 1966.[5]

The evolution of the *Horse* encompassed five distinct stages, as well as at least five additional studies and innumerable drawings of which only two are known through photographs. Its genesis culminated the intellectual probing and insistent extension of a conceptual apprehension of reality begun in *Baudelaire*. It began with two small versions of a *Horse and Rider* in which Duchamp-Villon again established a traditional theme as the basis of a modern restatement. The horse and rider is a stock image of Western art and the *Horse* is descended from the entire history of the equestrian monument. Through the ages equestrian monuments have summarized the qualities and values of their times, and the case is no less true with the *Horse*, an equestrian monument of the twentieth century. The repeated uses of tradition in Duchamp-Villon's work reflect a common strain in the thinking of the Puteaux artists. The Cubism of Picasso and Braque adhered to a conventional iconography of portraits, figures, and still lifes simply to facilitate its great formal innovations. At Puteaux a specific and concerted effort was launched to relate modernism with both the formal aims and epic themes of past art. Compositions of bathers, landscapes, city and harbor scenes, man's labors of harvesting and hunting, all themes intrinsic to a long history of French painting, pervaded the work of Gleizes, Metzinger, Léger, Delaunay and even Marcel Duchamp. The range of this iconography is not a half-understood blend of traditional and modern, but rather a profound synthesis of intellectual, social and aesthetic currents in a broad, historical panorama.

The rapidly modeled *Horse and Rider* sculptures parallel the initial stages of *Baudelaire, Maggy* and *The Lovers*. Like Degas' studies of the horse and rider, Duchamp-Villon's *Horse and Rider* is poised at the moment prior to the leap, in this case a metaphorical leap across the nineteenth century into the realities of a new age. In the first version, the horse is rendered in sections delineating the anatomy but alluding to mechanical functions. The mechanical transformation of the horse is clearly manifest in the second version. The rear haunches are ambiguously equated with the movement of the horse, but then, as the legs connect with the front quarters, the forms become steeled pistons set into a mechanical complex which forms the head and shoulders. The rider is also transformed as his legs merge with, and become an integral and functioning part of the pistons driving the horse. It is here that the old, literal image of horsepower assumes, through internal change and metamorphosis, the twentieth-century machine equation of horsepower, the basis for the final state of the *Horse*.

The next step in the work was more directly related to Duchamp-Villon's research of the preceding two years. In *Head of a Horse* he adapted the mechanical forms of *Horse and Rider* to a lucid distillation of tooled parts arranged schematically to complete the equation of horse-as-machine. The head is an important but comparatively little-known Cubist sculpture in which Duchamp-Villon realized an architectural network of forms bearing only minimal reference to observed phenomena. *Head of a Horse*, then, is ordered with the tensile strength of open forms interwoven by spatial voids, which extend the premises of constructed and fitted parts first realized in *Seated Girl*. It is apparent that this self-contained structural system gave a freedom of formal organization previously unknown in Cubist sculpture. The only comparable sculptures of the time were Picasso's cardboard and wood relief constructions of 1912–14, which had first extended collage elements into a real and tangible space and must be considered as a conceptual prototype. While the specific parts of the *Head of a Horse* were not retained in the final version, it did prepare the way for the elaborate intersection of machined forms of the *Horse*. It is, however, worth noting that the skeletal outlines of the head

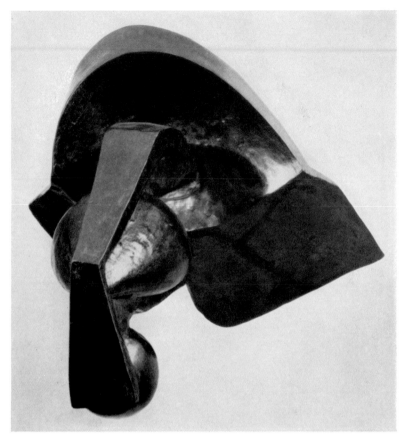

Fig. 63 *Head of a Horse.* 1914. Bronze, 19 in. high. The Joseph H. Hirshhorn Collection

can be compared with, and may have been suggested by, the bone structure of the flayed anatomy of a horse. The growth of the physical sciences and comparative anatomy in the second half of the nineteenth century made drawings of animal *écorchés* readily available in publications. The animal sculptor, Antoine Louis Barye (1796–1875), also made an intensive study of animal anatomy and his drawings of skeletal dissections were well known.

Although he was exempt from conscription due to the rheumatic fever he had suffered years before, Duchamp-Villon was determined to enlist when war was declared. He was accepted as a medical under-officer in the 11th Regiment of Cuirassiers and assigned to the hospital in St. Germain near Paris by the end of August.[6] The first stages of the

Horse had been tentatively formulated at that point, such as the beginning of the machined neck emerging in the *Small Horse*. As a cavalry officer, Duchamp-Villon became an expert rider, and was struck by the anachronism of the horse in a modern, mechanized war.[7] His involvement with the work and its final conception was hastened and intensified by his army experience, and in the fall the *Horse* was completed.

The final version combined and extended the several aspects of the earlier stages in a baroque multiplicity of views which makes the *Horse* one of the most intriguing and complex sculptures in the history of twentieth-century art. Through a superb balance of forces and plastic refinements we are given the visible transformation of the moving horse into the twentieth-century machine. To comprehend the act of transformation we must move around the *Horse* and perceive the change in a continuum of space and time. The metamorphosis of the natural into the man-made is achieved by fitting the long, sleek neck into the complex of pistons and shafts around which the potential thrust of the sculpture is centered. Seen from the left (fig. 67), the head appears capable of pivoting forward and back on the hinged joint formed by the two drive shafts connected to the central wheels, which were refinements of the mechanical elements in the second stage of the *Horse and Rider*. From a frontal position the locking pistons seem to propel

Fig. 64   *Very Small Horse.*
1914. Bronze, 3½ in. high.
Collection Mr. and Mrs.
Raymond Peter Pach

92

the horse forward. From the right side, the V-shaped shaft connects the three points with the hoof and is the unifying element which equates the horse's trot with the churning movement of a modern machine.

Moving around the sculpture, the neck rises from the linking machinery at its base and veers upward in a broad thrust. This aspect is perhaps the most dynamic in the sculpture and is what prompted Matisse, when he visited the studio in the fall of 1914, to characterize it as a "projectile." Duchamp-Villon was not sure the term was apt because a projectile is a man-made thing, with an uncomplicated line of flight; and he preferred to think of the varied rhythms of the horse's pacing and trotting.[8] The turn of the neck formed by triangular plates at the base was derived first from *Seated Girl*, and then the *Small Horse* as well as other, partial, studies (estate of the artist) which concentrated on details of this aspect.

The head, which curves back from the diagonal of the neck, is a concavity reminding one of the skeletal depressions of a horse's skull found in an *écorché* of the animal. This head reinforces the duality of animal and machine, suggesting the hybrid creations of Barye, which Duchamp-Villon knew well.[9] As in the fusion of composite elements in such ancient creatures as the sphinx and winged lion, Barye had joined together mythical forces in *Theseus Slaying the Centaur*, where the charged strength of the centaur is analogous to the thrust of the *Horse*. An even closer analogy exists between the hybrid quality of the *Horse* and Barye's *Roger and Angelica Mounted on the Hippogriffe*, both in conception and the similarity of the long, thin head and the hooked, nobbed nose of the hippogriffe to that of the *Horse*.

A fuller consideration of the sources of the equation of horse-qua-machine reveals the *Horse* as an extraordinary synthesis of a half-century of prevailing intellectual currents. Darwinian evolution stimulated an investigation of animal movement and comparative anatomy, from which emerged a unifying conception of the mechanical laws governing movement in all species. Muybridge's initial publication, *The Horse in Motion*, which appeared in 1872, was the first study of the sequential movement of the horse. Such works as Duhousset's *La machine animale* of 1873 and E. J. Marey's *Animal Mechanism*, published in New York in 1874, specifically compared the laws of animal movement to a manmade machine. In 1882, Leland Stanford, who had originally commissioned Muybridge's photographs of the horse, published a work by J. B. Stillman, also called *The Horse in Motion*. Stillman wrote, ". . . the study of the mechanical anatomy of the horse is a necessity . . . it will be found that the horse in motion is as perfectly harmonious in the display of his forces and their balance as a steam hammer."[10] He concluded that no creation of man could equal the "locomotive apparatus or machinery of the horse, with its compound system of levers, pulleys, tendons, springs and muscular powers."[11] Marey expanded the metaphor to a universal theory of comparative motion in his 1894 treatise, *Le Mouvement*. Duchamp-Villon knew the work of Muybridge and Marey, and may have been familiar with a few other pertinent studies.

The important point is that the equation of the horse as machine was well-established in the late nineteenth and early twentieth centuries.

The Futurists' assault on Paris was launched in 1909 with the publication of Marinetti's "Initial Manifesto of Futurism" in *Le Figaro* on February 20. In this and the other Futurist writings celebrating the twentieth century, the horse figured as the embodiment of dynamism and energy. Marinetti spoke of "broad-chested locomotives prancing on the rails, like huge steel horses bridled with long tubes," and one of the most famous doctrines, "thus a running horse has not four legs, but twenty, and their movements are triangular," was incorporated in Carlo Carrà's "Technical Manifesto of Futurist Painting" of 1910.[12]

Duchamp-Villon would have seen the pictorial equivalents of these images at the exhibition of Futurist painting at the Galerie Bernheim-Jeune in February 1912. Umberto Boccioni's painting of 1910–11, *The City Rises* (Museum of Modern Art, New York), portrayed an overpowering horse bursting across a cityscape with an uncontrollable force that matched the explosion of modern urban life on the contemporary sensibility. A profusion of robot horses, propelled by the strident rhythms of the city moved through Boccioni's *The Noise of the Street Penetrates the House* (Landesgalerie, Hanover). Another of Boccioni's runaway horses was that in the 1912 *Elasticity* (Collection Dr. Riccardo Jucker, Milan) in which a fragmented horse and rider hurtle through an urban landscape of smokestacks, factories and high-tension wires. However, this painting was not included in the Bernheim-Jeune exhibition and it cannot be established that Duchamp-Villon knew it. Given the attention the Futurists received in Paris, these images dramatized the possibilities inherent in an industrial, mechanized environment. The drawing of the horse (fig. 70) is infused with a distinct futuristic tone. But where the Italians invariably decomposed, splintered and multiplied the jarring forces of movement itself, Duchamp-Villon contained mechanical forms with an instinctive French lucidity and refinement. The spiral intersection of the neck and, in a modified form, the armature of the hind quarters, in this drawing appear again in the *Horse*, but are even more decisively tempered by a distilled plasticity and formalism, essentially alien to the Futurists' shattered pictorial effects.

Boccioni began to work with sculpture in the spring of 1912, and at that time, while in Paris, he visited the studios of Brancusi, Agero, Archipenko and Duchamp-Villon.[13] The next year he exhibited his sculpture in Paris at Galerie La Boétie from June 20 to July 16. While certain similarities of conception with Duchamp-Villon's existed, a distinct gulf between their plastic realizations emerged. Among the works exhibited was *Unique Forms of Continuity in Space* (Museum of Modern Art, New York), a fragmented, striding figure with a pictorial interpenetration of space and volume, which may have deliberately revamped Duchamp-Villon's *Torso of a Young Man*. It is this literal, almost random, interpenetration of disparate objects, which Boccioni stressed in the preface of the catalog for the exhibition, that distinguishes the formal means of

Fig. 65 *Horse*. 1914.
Bronze, 40 in. high.
Collection, The Museum
of Modern Art, New York.
Van Gogh Purchase Fund

his sculpture from those of Duchamp-Villon. Boccioni also stressed the end of sculpture as predominantly architectural, which may reflect the influence of Duchamp-Villon's writings and Boccioni's visit to Puteaux. In turn, the emphasis placed by Boccioni on the concept of simultaneity and the continuity of sculpture in space may have affected Duchamp-Villon's resolution of the transition from the organic to the mechanical in the *Horse*. It is the spiral course of Boccioni's *Development of a Bottle in Space* (Museum of Modern Art, New York) moving up and around a formal center that reflects a concept indirectly related to the unfurling of Duchamp-Villon's *Horse*; only this particular

95

Fig. 66 *Horse*

aspect of Boccioni's sculpture can be profitably compared with Duchamp-Villon's work. In sum, it was the example of the Futurists' proclamation of certain ideas, rather than a formal usage as such, which should be examined in the context of Duchamp-Villon's major work. Duchamp-Villon and the Puteaux artists were aware, even slightly defensive, of the issues raised by Futurism. André Salmon, in the catalog preface to the joint exhibition of Duchamp-Villon, Gleizes, Villon and Metzinger held at the Galerie André Groult in 1914, spoke for the four when he stated that Futurism was "literary" in its origins, and had borrowed from Cubism for its means.

96

The machine aesthetic at Puteaux took many divergent forms, and was reflected in the writings of Léger, Delaunay, Picabia, Mercereau and Barzun, as well as Duchamp-Villon. In addition to the distilled plasticity of machined parts used by Léger and Duchamp-Villon, specific landmarks of the modern urban landscape appeared, such as the Eiffel Tower, the subject of the series Robert Delaunay began in 1910. For Delaunay and Duchamp-Villon, the Eiffel Tower was the most dramatic symbol and accomplishment of revolutionary technology and engineering. Duchamp-Villon hailed the Tower as miraculous and of an unsurpassed beauty, likening it to Notre Dame as a twentieth-century cathedral.[14] Events which signified human achievement made possible by the machine were recorded; Delaunay paid tribute to the first flight across the English Channel in his painting of 1914, *Hommage à Blériot*, filled with swirling motors and propellers. Paintings of composite industrial landscapes were common, as in Gleizes' *Passy*, 1912 (Museum des 20 Jahrhunderts, Vienna) and *La Ville et le Fleuve* of 1913 (Solomon R. Guggenheim Museum, New York), or of the visual dynamics of the city as in Picabia's 1911 *Paris* (Collection Maria Martins, Rio de Janeiro).

The Puteaux artists frequently contrasted a traditional motif against a modern setting, implying a space-time continuum, a prototype which reappears in the transition from the nineteenth to twentieth centuries in the *Horse*. In a painting which forecast Duchamp-Villon's experience in the war, Roger de la Fresnaye's *Artillery* (the Florene May Schoenborn and Samuel Marx Collection, New York) of 1911 depicted a cavalry officer moving incongruously among the armored weapons of modern warfare. Gleizes juxtaposed a group of classical nudes in *The Bathers* of 1912 (Musée National d'Art Moderne, Paris) against a landscape which shifts from a soft, rolling hillside to a harsh urban background of factories and smokestacks rendered in severe Cubist planes. A more specific metamorphosis was achieved by Jean Marchand that year in the *Bathers* (whereabouts unknown), where three nudes are in an idyllic rural landscape set against a metallic background of bridges, wires and trains. Perhaps the most dramatic and monumental contrast of old and new was Delaunay's 1912 *Ville de Paris* (Musée National d'Art Moderne, Paris), where the three Graces are seen in front of the Eiffel Tower and a cityscape shattered by forces of the contemporary world.

By 1914 the horse had appeared with mechanical overtones in the work of the Puteaux circle. In La Fresnay's *Le Cuirassier* (Musée National d'Art Moderne, Paris) a horse of sharp Cubist outlines and charged power dominated the composition. Gleizes depicted several horses with arched, sweeping necks in his 1912 painting *The Hunt* (Collection Edouard Labouchère, Paris) which may have partially suggested Duchamp-Villon's treatment of the *Horse*. Although not specifically mechanical, a sculpture made by Delaunay in the summer of 1913, and exhibited that fall at the Erster Deutscher Herbstsalon, invoked sensations of movement. It was called *Cheval: Sculpture simultanée* (now destroyed; reproduced Michel Seuphor, *L'Art Abstrait*, Paris, 1949, p. 45) and consisted of a small wooden hobbyhorse about two and a half feet high, painted in bril-

Fig. 67
Horse

liant Orphist hues intended to convey movement through the simultaneous interaction of the colors. The horse itself was uninventive, but is of great interest because the idea for a sculpture of a simultaneous horse originated with Apollinaire, who passed it on to Duchamp-Villon, Gleizes, Marcel Duchamp and Léger, as well as to Delaunay, in the Spring of 1913.[15] Delaunay was the only one to act immediately on the idea, but it may well have planted the seeds of inspiration for Duchamp-Villon's sculpture.

Concern for the mechanistic and the forces of motion in the immediate circle of the family played a telling role in creating the atmosphere from which the *Horse* emerged. The Duchamp brothers were very close, and as Duchamp-Villon related, they were each

Fig. 68   *Horse*

other's severest critics.[16] Duchamp had been fascinated by movement and the machine since 1911 when, at Raymond's request, he had painted a coffee grinder with its handle seen in various positions simultaneously, for the decoration of his brother's kitchen. His series of paintings beginning with the *Chess Players*, *Nude Descending the Staircase* and the *Bride* of 1911–12 (all Philadelphia Museum of Art) explored a myriad complex of mechanical and robotlike forms. Villon also became increasingly involved with a machine aesthetic. His painting of 1914, *Atelier de Mécanique* (Collection Edwin Nevin, New York), consisted of a broad panorama of machine-shop activities which seem to emanate from a rotating flywheel at the right of the canvas. This flywheel mechanism is virtually identical to the apparatus found in Duchamp-Villon's drawing (fig. 70) which is similarly a generative wellspring used to propel and unfurl the horse across the open space.

Among the many topics discussed at Puteaux was the philosophy of Henri Bergson (1859–1941), whose thought strongly affected the group. Bergson's philosophy, particularly as found in *Creative Evolution* of 1907, established a conceptual base for the progressive states of Duchamp-Villon's mature work. Bergson stressed the reality of evolution as a state of transition, the true state of existence being change itself. Each new form flows out of previous forms, adding something new, but explained as much by prior states as it explains them. Evolution of a form is a process of accumulated knowledge which prolongs the past state while transforming the new state. The process of flux in the *Horse* embodies this conception as the sculpture, at each turn, is informed by past states fusing with and being transformed by new states of knowledge.

Bergson's thinking also contributed to the idea of simultaneity, in wide currency by 1914, and it influenced Duchamp-Villon. Simultaneity first derived from Cézanne's use of shifting perspectives,[17] and later from the incorporation of multiple views of an object seen from several sides by the Cubists. The time element in this synthesis led to the use of the idea of the Fourth Dimension, first postulated by Apollinaire.[18] The term appeared in the forward to the Futurists' 1912 exhibition and by the end of the year had been applied to a wide range of pictorial devices. It included not only objects seen from all sides at once but objects widely separated in time and space, a device particularly important to the Puteaux artists. The Futurists employed it to show moving objects colliding and merging, and in 1912 Delaunay extended the idea to the simultaneous interaction of colored discs. Henri-Martin Barzun developed it as a form of poetry which brought together disparate sensory reactions unique to the rhythms of the modern world. Barzun also stated that he found a plastic equivalent for his ideas in Duchamp-Villon's work when he visited him in 1915.[19] In the *Horse*, Duchamp-Villon unified two aspects of simultaneity in a way unique to sculpture at that time. He first constructed a series of multiple perspectives in the intersections of the head, base and neck to effect a passage through time and space. Within this passage, the fusion of animal and machine, conceived as being separate and distant, encompasses a second aspect of simultaneity.

Duchamp-Villon wrote that he wished to explore areas of plasticity previously unknown,[20] and the *Horse* fulfilled this ambition. It marks, along with *Head of a Horse*, the emergence of a Cubist sculpture as complex and subtle as Cubist painting yet determined by purely sculptural terms, independent of all painterly associations. Only Archipenko's *Boxers* of 1914 (Solomon R. Guggenheim Museum, New York) was of parallel complexity based on a sculptural realization of Cubist principles, and, significantly, its turning figures bear a certain similarity to the intersecting plates of the base of the *Horse*. Cubist sculpture was slow to capitalize on the freedom from painterly con-

Fig. 69 *Large Horse*. 1914. Bronze, 54 in. high. Collection Louis Carré

ventions won by Duchamp-Villon and Archipenko. Lipchitz did not achieve a comparable autonomy until the mid-1920s, when he arrived at an incorporation of Cubist principles divorced from painting. In a sense, Laurens never achieved it. Picasso and Gonzales extended its implications in their wire constructions of the 1930s. Duchamp-Villon's architectural conception of sculpture, realized through the principles of Cubism, was at

Fig. 70 Drawing for
Horse. c. 1914. Charcoal.
Dimensions and where-
abouts unknown

Fig. 71 Drawing for
Horse. c. 1914. Charcoal.
Dimensions and where-
abouts unknown

the heart of a profound alteration of sculpture in this century. By breaking from the carved monolith and creating a sculpture that could be composed, designed, constructed and assembled with the flexibility of collage, Duchamp-Villon helped to reverse, like Cubist painting itself, the entire Renaissance tradition. The new freedom thus secured for sculpture reverberated at many depths. Brancusi, who had taken the closed monolithic form to its ultimate conclusion, realized the consequences of the open network of assembled forms, and applied them to his wood sculpture. Beginning with the 1914 *Prodigal Son* (Philadelphia Museum of Art), Brancusi explored an entirely new range of formal means. The entire Constructivist tradition stems from the new conception, and at its full extension effected the oeuvre of David Smith, the great heir to the new vocabulary launched in 1914. Duchamp-Villon, with Picasso, Archipenko and Brancusi, stands as a precursor of a sculptural freedom and a new tradition the full consequences of which we have yet to see.

1. "The power of the machine imposes itself and we scarcely conceive living beings any more without it. We are strangely moved by the rapid brushing by of men and things and we accustom ourselves without knowing it to perceive the forces of the former through the forces they dominate. From that to an opinion of life in which it appears to us simply under its form of higher dynamism there is only a step, which is quickly made." Letter reprinted in *Pach*, p. 19.

2. "L'architecture et le fer," *Poème et Drame*, VII, January–March 1914, p. 23. Reprinted, p. 114.

3. Golding, *op. cit.*, p. 109, has suggested that the first studies were started in late 1913, but offers no supporting evidence. Pach, in *Masters of Modern Art*, p. 112, states that they were begun "about a year before the war." However, in view of his other projects of 1913–14, the most prolific period of his life, and since none of the studies were exhibited during that time, a date of early 1914 for the inception of the sculpture seems most likely.

4. Pach, *Queer Thing, Painting*, p. 144.

5. According to his brothers, Duchamp-Villon expressed his wish to enlarge the sculpture. Walter Pach also reported the artist's wishes to Alfred H. Barr, Jr. However, no written instructions have survived. The first enlargement was carried out under Villon's direction, the second under Duchamp. Duchamp-Villon also wished to do a "definitive version in steel" (Pach, *Masters of Modern Art*, p. 111).

6. Letter to Walter Pach, August 10, 1914.

7. Pach, *Queer Thing, Painting*, p. 144.

8. *Ibid.*, p. 145.

9. *Ibid.*

10. Leland Stanford, *The Horse in Motion*, Boston, 1882, p. 13.

11. *Ibid.*, p. 19.

12. Published in Filippo Marinetti, *Le Futurisme*, Paris, 1911.

13. Reported by Madame Duchamp-Villon to Marcel Duchamp; see also Gino Severini, *Tutta la vita di un pittore*, Rome, 1946, p. 163.

14. Raymond Duchamp-Villon, *op. cit.* Reprinted, p. 114.

15. Guillaume Apollinaire, "Chronique Mensuelle," *Soirées de Paris*, 15 November 1913, p. 2. See also Robert Delaunay, *Du Cubisme à l'Art Abstrait*, Paris, 1957, pp. 136, 139.

16. Pach, *Queer Thing, Painting*, p. 147.

17. See George Heard Hamilton, "Cézanne, Bergson and The Image of Time," *College Art Journal*, New York, 1956, pp. 2–13.

18. First in *Gil Blas*, November 26, 1911, and then in *Les Peintres Cubistes*, Paris, 1913.

19. Henri-Martin Barzun, "La révolution polyrythmique moderne," *Poème et Drame*, September–October, 1913, p. 4.

20. Letter to Walter Pach, February 26, 1915. Reprinted in *Pach*, p. 22.

26.   Le Coq (Rooster)
1916. Painted plaster. 17⅛ × 14⅝ in.
The Phillips Collection, Washington, D.C. Bequest of Katherine Dreier
Exh.: 1917, Society of Independent Artists, New York; 1919, Salon
d'Automne; 1925, Galerie Vavin-Raspail (bronze); 1929, Brummer Gallery;
1931, Galerie Pierre

In September 1915, Duchamp-Villon was transferred from his hospital post at St. Germain to the front at Champagne. He could no longer return to his studio, and increasingly he felt the painful separation from artistic and intellectual life. He had been sure—as had been so many of his countrymen—that the war would be over within three months, ended by a decisive victory over the Germans.[1] Instead it dragged on, leaving him isolated, his sensibilities enervated.

He could do little work, and was able to complete only two sculptures before his death in 1918; one being this painted medallion. Executed as an ornament for a theater set up at the front to entertain the troops, Duchamp-Villon felt, because of his audience, he could not depart to any great extent from naturalistic conventions.[2]

The circumstances which dictated the informal and decorative qualities of the work made it impossible to consider the relief on the same critical level as the rest of his oeuvre. In 1917 Duchamp-Villon sent the medallion to Walter Pach in New York, where it was exhibited that fall.

1. Letter to Walter Pach, August 10, 1914.
2. Letter to Walter Pach, January 5, 1917.

Fig. 72 *Rooster*. 1916. Painted plaster, 17⅛ × 14⅝ in. The Phillips Collection, Washington, D.C.
Bequest of Katherine Dreier

Fig. 73   *Portrait of Professor
Gosset.* 1918. Bronze, 4 in. high.
Collection Marcel Duchamp

Fig. 74   *Portrait of Professor Gosset.* 1918. Bronze,
11¾ in. high. Albright-Knox Art Gallery, Buffalo

27.   Portrait of Professor Gosset
1918. Bronze. 4 in. high
Collection Marcel Duchamp, New York

Large version. 11¾ in. high
Albright-Knox Art Gallery, Buffalo
Exh.: 1919, Salon d'Automne; 1929, Brummer Gallery; 1931, Galerie Pierre

While stationed at Champagne in late 1916 Duchamp-Villon contracted typhoid fever and was confined to the military hospital at Mourmelon. The fever lasted well into 1917 and when it had abated he was left completely debilitated. He was forced into a long period of recuperation during which time his condition varied; but he was able to accomplish physical activity only with the greatest effort. He managed to do some writing, including "Variations de la connaissance pendant le travail d'art," and a short comedy, *Les Sémaphores*, written in collaboration with Jean Keller and performed for the troops.

On May 20, 1918, Duchamp-Villon wrote to Pach that despite his weakness he had been able to progress quite far on a small portrait of one of the doctors who was attending him.[1] This portrait of Professor Gosset was Duchamp-Villon's final sculpture. Although it was made under the most trying conditions, one can discern ideas long present in his work. The stark reductions of *Baudelaire* and *Maggy* are continued, now distilled to a point analogous to a Brancusi head. The portrait consists of two distinct parts, each clearly articulated, which appear to have been joined or fitted together around the seam of the mask, and which thus create their own order and logic of existence. The image and method of construction forecast Picasso's sculpted heads of 1931.

In retrospect, one cannot help but see in the bare, skeletal outlines a premonition of his impending fate. In the months following the completion of the portrait, Duchamp-Villon's strength slowly waned, and he was finally unable to withstand an attack of blood poisoning. He died on October 7, 1918, in the Cannes military hospital. This last work is all the more disquieting for the slim clues it provides to the direction his work might have taken. He had been sure he would not die young, that he would live to accomplish what he had set out to achieve.[2] That his achievement, if only partially realized, had nevertheless helped to alter the course of sculpture in this century, makes his death all the more a tragic irony.

1. Reprinted in *Pach*, p. 25. Although the work has been dated 1917, this letter would indicate 1918 as the correct date.
2. Roosevelt, *op. cit.*

Raymond Duchamp-Villon in his uniform of the 11th Regiment of Cuirasseurs, St. Germain, 1917

Writings by Duchamp-Villon

Draft of an Article on the Salon d'Automne of 1911

"Projet d'article sur le Salon d'Automne de 1911."

Whether Duchamp-Villon intended this article for publication is not clear. It was probably drafted in response to the controversy that had arisen over the Cubist painters who were shown together at the 1911 Salon d'Automne. As vice-president of the sculpture jury and a member of the hanging committee, Duchamp-Villon was instrumental in persuading the Salon officials to exhibit the work of Gleizes, Metzinger, Léger, Delaunay, Marcel Duchamp, Jacques Villon, La Fresnaye and Lhote as a group in Salle VII. The article repeated the earlier group manifestation at the Indépendants, and although Picasso and Braque did not exhibit at either, the two Salons together gave the public their first extensive view of Cubism. The reaction was predictably hostile, and many critical reviews which discussed Cubism for the first time were generally misguided and uninformed. Amid the confusion surrounding the Cubists, Duchamp-Villon attempted to interject a rational analysis, particularly in relation to the historical position of the movement. He was also obviously distressed at the omission of any mention of sculpture, and, as one seeking to restore the art to its former prominence, he dwelt on its different conception, execution and means of comprehension.

The public is attracted here as elsewhere by the paintings and examines with less attention the numerous interesting works of sculpture. However, the works are present in the rooms among the glass cases and paintings in the tradition of the Salon d'Automne where fortunately the depressing cemetery of marbles and plasters has been eliminated.

We must attribute this apparent indifference to the austerity of an art which does not put itself forward and which one must sympathize with in order to understand. Statuary would not be able to impress the public: more than all the other plastic arts, sculpture lends itself to reflection by speaking to the mind through its own means. This technique is seldom familiar to the spectator for whom the artist often shows too little concern. For a long time, in fact, sculptors have not had faith in sculpture. Except for some exceptional talents in the nineteenth century, hundreds upon hundreds of statues have accumulated which the weight of time already crushes, for they are powerless to prevail.

To what do we attribute this failure if not to the sole desire to please and to flatter public opinion by proposing to it average, well-made works whose great fault is to remain commonplace. If a sale is assured, then it is a success: it is also early death and well-deserved oblivion for works without a lofty purpose, whose author thought only of himself.

This misunderstanding will continue as long as public opinion requires that sculpture be immediately accessible to it: for the less an art form demands of the intelligence, the more it offers to the senses, and the best that sort has to offer is a grossly imitative sensation.

The spirit and the letter are still in conflict here, and unfortunately for our age, statuary, save for some rare exceptions, remains indifferent to this struggle which should interest it very much. Technique is nothing. Sculpture, like painting, like music, can find a world of special harmonies whose origin is also in nature. Mistress of three dimensions, sculpture has as her servants line, plane, and volume. And life with its balance, its cadences, its rhythms provides her themes.

Raymond Duchamp-Villon

Manuscript Notes (from the Estate of the artist)

Parts I and II are from the same document, but the order is uncertain. The sharply critical tone of Part II indicates that the article may in fact have been intended as a personal clarification rather than as a public statement.

Part I

It [the public at the Salon d'Automne] has had to learn some simple, essential truths which artists have ignored for a long time now, to understand that art is not a matter of business and that a work can displease and be beautiful, while another which pleases cannot be [beautiful].

The public now knows that plastic harmony is infinite, like musical harmony, and that with some effort the imagination can enjoy it as a conquest of the unknown.

Artists always have taken pains to develop knowledge of limitless harmonies, but never until now had there been such a burst of research. One would think that after having been repressed for centuries it suddenly found a way into the light, although not entirely coherently. Every kind of vision, every talent, has been employed and if what the Salon d'Automne has offered us until now has been full of interest, this is only the beginning of a triumphant leap toward the truth of which the faults are countless.

Part II

The Salon d'Automne (unpublished draft)

A few words must be said about those who have wrongly been called Cubists. A whole room has been set aside for them, the atmosphere of which is distinctly different from the rest of the Salon. None is like another, yet they share the same idea. This is a somewhat brutal reaction against an excess of sensibility in an attempt to achieve a more profound understanding of life while intentionally rejecting truth to appearance. Rightly or wrongly? Time will tell, for the work now on trial is not definite enough to convince us. Merely to mention, in this room alone, Le Fauconnier, La Fresnaye whose landscapes are not at all provocative, Gleizes and Léger who are decorators in spite of themselves, Lhote whose picture of the port of Bordeaux is clear and sober, Marcel Duchamp (rejected; he is still a bit hesitant) whose intentions are insufficiently realized, Segonzac, lively but dry . . .

Although these notes were probably not directly connected with the Salon article, they probably stem from the issues raised at that time. The discussion of the arguments centering around Cubism, which Duchamp-Villon mentions in Parts III and IV, coincides with the controversy over the 1911 Salon d'Automne. Parts VI and VII are less specifically related to these arguments, but they probably date from no more than two years later. Part V contains a succinct outline of Duchamp-Villon's essential goals, and, in the context of the historical sense revealed in Part VI, is an outline of his mature theoretical approach.

Part III

I don't believe that one can offer a satisfying explanation of an art form, whatever the perspective of time may be, and the assurance it gives of avoiding mistakes. Certain remarkable men have devoted themselves to the problem, and others to each work by each of the great artists and each of the schools now considered classic. But this doesn't prevent each of us from studying them and understanding them in our own way, which has nothing to do with theirs. Today the violent discussions which accompanied the appearance of Cubism are the same which disturbed our fathers in the great days of Impressionism; they recur every time remarkable personalities must assert themselves. The key to the problem is right there, rather than in ingenious theories: the feeling for art arises from the encounter in a work of art of two personalities, the artist's and the spectator's. This does not necessarily imply any communion between them. Quite to the contrary, there is a violent collision between the one's conventional learning and the other's spontaneity. But the effective presence of the creator in his work is the indication and proof of its value. That's exactly why I could, at the beginning and without knowing them, be attracted by the Cubist painters, and that's why little by little I could understand their aesthetic and better appreciate it . . .

Part IV

The emergence of a new style is essential today. Although expected by everyone, it has not yet appeared despite remarkable exertions, apparently contradictory but which actually are no more than the oscillations preceding a state of equilibrium.

Art Nouveau, which has been so much maligned, had the advantage of first posing the question and of providing solutions which, although rarely satisfactory, were instructive and fruitful.

Part V

The sole purpose of the arts is neither description nor imitation but the creation of unknown beings from elements which are always present but not apparent.

Part VI

Plastic art is no longer solely concerned with what in life is visible; it tries to realize the process of thought. The whole difficulty is in adapting its techniques to this new conception.

The problem is to reveal the vibration of thought itself and thereby to provoke states of consciousness hitherto unexpected or unknown. Only yesterday an artist, when in front of nature, reflected it in his work, as it were, with a more or less delicate eye, a more or less luminous vision. But such work was only indirectly concerned with the intelligence. This was the origin of Impressionism. After that, Neo-Impressionism revived the formula by adding a scientific purpose which enlarged its technique without changing its spirit. The school of sensitivity (*i.e.*, Cubism) first broke with this tradition of decomposed light. By seeking simple harmonies of muted colors, and by studying nature through the relation of objects, this school, itself reacting against a riot of color, and by its extreme subtleties, provoked the recent studies in composition, and experiments in the harmony of volumes and arabesques, experiments which were serious, profound, and always striving for sensibility. It seems that today we should achieve an effort of will capable of translating the power of life in action. Compositions and landscapes are deliberately planned, and nature plays no part other than as a means of execution. Pushed to the extreme this tendency ends in the audacities of quasi-geometric synthesis and in the fragmentation of objects, leaving to the imagination the task of recreating the equilibrium.

Part VII

A finished work is no more than a recollection of our efforts, and it is just such efforts that we prize in it. Could one then separate effort from the force that engendered it, which is indeed the vitality of a personality? There is no single phenomenon capable of balancing, by the satisfactions it provides, the joy of developing an idea from its germination until the complete accomplishment of the act of creation; neither the difficulty nor the pain, nor the suffering, can make one forget the happiness and honor of creating. Should one expect more of a work accomplished in collaboration with others, and should the imagination seek its reward when the idea is approved by others? No, if the opinion of the result so obtained should be increased by this fact; yes, if one must consider one's work as a stranger to oneself, as in some way abandoned to a higher collective thought which itself does not create but provokes creation.

A Reply to an Inquiry about Carpeaux's "La Danse" at the Opera

["Réponse à une enquête au sujet de *La Danse* de Carpeaux à l'Opéra."
First half published in *Gil Blas*, September 17, 1912.]

The first half of this manuscript was published as a reply to an inquiry circulated by the critic Louis Vauxcelles regarding the proposed removal of the Carpeaux *La Danse* for reasons of its preservation. It is in some ways the most important extant document pertaining to Duchamp-Villon, for not only is it the most extended and specific statement of his sculptural aims, but it reveals his lively and conscientious involvement in the pertinent matters of the day as well. Its considered treatment of the problem is typical of his historical awareness tempered by a concern for practical considerations.

Dear Sir,

Despite my wish to answer at some length an inquiry whose subject interests me very much, I am unable to find the spare time necessary to give my ideas some kind of form.

We suffer, or rather sculpture suffers, from museum sickness. What was not there, we wish to put there, and whatever is done we wish to store there. It is an absurdity which gradually turns sculptors from their art: they become modelers of bibelots, enlarged to monuments or reduced to clock figures as need be. That and other causes contribute to separate us from the true goal of sculpture which is above all architectural. There are numerous examples of remarkable works which look deplorable in the open air. Our age, which created some very beautiful objects for the interior, produces nothing which can hold its own outside.

They are all guilty, the State which builds not at all or badly, the architects who build copies; also, but to a lesser degree, the artists who do not act.

What should outdoor sculpture be in our time, and in our climate? Who could say? We must feel our way, make many mistakes, for a long time, perhaps, before obtaining results. There is a whole education to be carried on—we can at the most summarize the qualities to be achieved in a rather meager formula: SEEN FROM A DISTANCE THE WORK MUST LIVE AS A DECORATION THROUGH THE HARMONY OF VOLUMES, PLANES, AND LINES—, the subject being of little or no importance at all.

A work was conceived for a particular site; once there, it is appropriately lighted, its proportions have been fixed in an appropriate relationship with the surroundings. All that can't be taken away with it. We obviously eliminate much of its attraction by burying it, as you say so well, in the graveyard of a museum. I do not know the state of the group in question, "La Danse," but it is hard for me to think that no effective protection could be tried. To transfer it to the Louvre is an easy way to solve a problem which certainly has other solutions. What is needed is a little ingenuity; that no doubt is what discourages our wonderful administration! Your initiative will perhaps move them to take some action. Let us hope so.

It is, however, disturbing from another point of view, that a decorative work of this importance is, after forty years of exposure, in such a bad state that there is already concern about its preservation. We might suspect a lack of foresight in its construction. That is possible and ought to be considered. But what is certain is that sculpture conceived like Carpeaux's group is made to be sheltered and that it has none of the characteristics of outdoor architectural sculpture. That does not detract at all from its intrinsic merit, and criticism is directed rather at the architect of the monument who did not place it appropriately. All young sculptors now work with acquisition by the State in mind: for them this sort of department-store museum will house their work which is conceived for the museum. When by chance the opportunity arises to decorate or create a monument, it is impossible for the sculptor to reeducate himself. Thus, for some time now in France, we have lost the feeling for outdoor sculpture, which is the only sculpture of interest. Our statues in public squares, enlarged bibelots, in small replicas make delightful clock figures; and centerpieces would easily make, by an inverse process, fashionable garden decorations.

This aberration results from the fact that we use statuary very little in architecture or that we reserve it for decoration with no relationship to the structure decorated.

A statue here, a medallion there, farther along a basket of fruit, and the architect goes to sleep happy. The pose or the style of the figures he uses matters little; nor does it matter if they have been conceived to decorate an apartment. The scaling down will make its proportions harmonize with the surroundings and all will be well and good. That was Garnier's error in the group of "La Danse" which has none of the characteristics of outdoor sculpture and which ought to be sheltered to resist time. Less than fifty years have sufficed to prove it.

It is rather difficult to define what modern outdoor sculpture ought to be. It seems to me that we can summarize the desired qualities in this formula: TO LIVE AT A DISTANCE (I mean to live as decoration through the harmony of volumes, planes, and lines). So far as I know, only Rude's *Chant du Dèpart* fulfills this requirement.

Raymond Duchamp-Villon

The Eiffel Tower (*written in 1913*)

[Published in part, as "L'architecture et le fer," *Poème et Drame*, VII (January–March 1914), pp. 22–29.]

This article, along with the more famous section of the January 16, 1913 letter to Pach on the "power of the machine," is one of the most revealing documents on the impact of the machine on modern art and life to be found in early twentieth-century literature. It unites poetic fantasy with a wide range of learning in modern architecture, a fusion of sensibility and intellect typical of Duchamp-Villon's temperament. For the artists at Puteaux, especially Duchamp-Villon and Delaunay, the Eiffel Tower was, despite almost universal public derision, a symbol of the dynamism and beauty of the modern urban world. It appeared in Delaunay's paintings and was a constant symbol in the simultaneous poetry of Henri-Martin Barzun, a member of the Puteaux group and founder of *Poème et Drame*, a magazine dedicated to the new art forms celebrating contemporary life. The new materials, such as concrete, discussed in the article were employed by Duchamp-Villon in his 1913 architectural reliefs, the *Dog, Cat, Doves* and *Parrot*. He also intended to cast a definitive version of the *Horse* in steel as an ultimate statement of its modernity. The forms, if not the materials, used by Duchamp-Villon in his architectural projects were influenced by his friend, the architect Auguste Perret, the most important pioneer in the use of structural reinforced concrete. Perret was also undoubtedly influential in Duchamp-Villon's concern with the relation of architecture to the modern world.

The article as printed in *Poème et Drame* was the same, with the exception of the background material on modern architecture, which was omitted.

It is said that they are going to issue new stamps of the Eiffel Tower. Now doesn't this mean a confession of injustice and a desire for reparation? Had it been built in America, it would have been overwhelmed with publicity and hyperbole; in France we have ridiculed it: different systems of education, but the same results. Fortunately time eliminates the follies of men and, no matter what they may say, ridicule never destroys anything but the false and the weak. The Tower continues to trace against the changing skies its gray silhouette and golden head, and to raise on high its lace-like geometry, like a desire, like a fixed symbol. As for the critics and scholars responsible for this undeserved discredit, no doubt they will continue to explode a new bomb each day under the illusion that they are spreading light. It is not any the less distressing that because of their incompetence public opinion has for such a long time scorned the art of metal work and has seen in it only gross, vulgar utility, the result of ingenious and thorough calculations.

Thus we did not see, nor dared to defend against conjecture, a work of great power and daring, a fantastic hall proclaiming the glory of steel, the Galerie des Machines constructed for the exposition of 1889. The memory of it dominates our first notions of collective life, and I still recall very clearly, in the bright light of that immense interior, an hallucinatory walk as if along a bridge rolling over the flying whirlpools, the serpentine belts, amidst the roaring, the whistles and the sirens, passing above black holes, discs, pyramids, and cubes. I must admit, to my shame, that I have for Dutert, who created such a work, an appreciation and respect that the École Militaire cannot make me forget.

This destructive attitude, disguised by arguments of public aesthetics, is proof of the indifference in which architecture in metal is held. However, is there not a surprising similarity between the conceptions of engineers working in steel and those of medieval masons? Is there not the same desire to form spaces where people may circulate at ease, the same need to develop lightness and simplicity to the point of paradox?

Do we not find in both the same boundless ambition always to achieve the greater, the taller, the more daring? Across from Gothic Notre-Dame, the true tower of modern Paris rises on the Champ de Mars. Both works, the tower and the nave, are born of the same desire to build and both fulfill a similar dream of superhuman exaltation.

It is true, no doubt, that construction in metal alone is but a transitional phase. We must nonetheless preserve the monuments which have crowned it, and pay homage to the pioneers who dared at a time when there was great risk.

First of all, we must mention the Labrouste brothers to whom we owe the halls of the Bibliothèque Nationale and of the Bibliothèque Sainte-Geneviève. They were built about 1850, yet we have never praised their elegance and simplicity, impossible to achieve in other materials. In these temples of learning, one has to see the bold columns spread their fluted skin beneath the vault and effortlessly bear the crisp arches. Around them is an atmosphere of calm and grandeur, the very sign of style, and truly it is painful to study the errors of those who have not understood this lesson.

We must also mention Baltard who knew how to give to the Halles, solely through the logical development of their use and needs, the appearance of a mysterious organism always on the alert, containing during the night the activity of the city in order to return it sharpened anew for the morrow. Broad alley-ways, stalls, no obstacles; it is a temporary shelter which must constantly be rebuilt, the void which can never remain empty: one of the most remarkable monuments by virtue of its adaptation and its function, the primary condition of an architecture worthy of the name. Later I was told that the Pont des Arts was the first example of iron construction, toward 1811. You will forgive me for only mentioning this, for I plan to complete the details, if this study is to be published. Surely this is the origin of our modern architecture which complements the contributions of iron with those of concrete.

But this is neither the time nor the place to develop this thesis. We all know the few examples of liberated architecture which Paris owes to it, and we need but dream a bit to foresee the future of reinforced concrete, combined with stone, marble or even wooden decoration. The steel skeleton allows all kinds of daring, the most robust as well as the most delicate. Let us do justice to it and, when it deserves, grant its merit as a work of art.

Everyone remembers, at least from pictures, the substantial remains left here and there by those geniuses of masonry, the Romans, and no one challenges, for example, the highest acclaim given in the almanac of national glories to what remains of the Pont du Gard. And yet its *raison d'être* was entirely utilitarian, as is today the Garabit viaduct launched between two mountains, spanning in one stroke a space where the Arc de Triomphe could be placed on the towers of Notre-Dame. Such an achievement could not be reduced to the value of the Argenteuil bridge, a *work* of art. To adapt a technique to the nature and the proportions of the surrounding countryside is to solve architectural problems. Eiffel, perhaps without suspecting so, at that moment as well as later, obeyed exigencies of formal order controlled and supported by the logic of materials. This is the best situation for the preparation and completion of a masterpiece—this ignorance of classified artistic ideas and laws, which allows the artist the joy of creating according to a preconceived ideal.

Eiffel, an architect without knowing it, was a genius. He alone, at the end of the last century admired French architecture and could translate into simple lines its daring strength and grace. The magnificent tower, owing its preservation to a sham utility, at first passed for the wager of a fanatic believer.

As a baptism, it received, like all new things, its nonsensically inept certificate duly signed by the leading pundits of the day: certain witty artists even circulated a protest from people of taste which was called the Protest of the 300 Masters. The ingenious François Coppèe expressed his scorn by exclaiming: "You can go up for 10 cents!" At the same time they were making ironic comments in the provinces: on a triumphal arch erected at the Tour de Peilz for the vine-growers' festival, one could read:

> These peaceful pastoral regions
> Appreciate the hand of time
> The Eiffel Tower is 300 meters high
> Our Tower is 600 years old.

On street-corners they made fun of it in verse whose exaggerated grace can be appreciated in this passage:

> And they say that from on high
> One will see to the Congo
> Brazza chasing the gazelle
> From the Tour Eiffel.

Edouard Lockroy, then a minister, had the courage to protest officially against these jokes, but at the time no voice was heard to explain the beauty of such a creation. The statistics and examples, which amused the public, were not intended to disguise the notion of a rather mad although successful experiment. Some of these explanations are rather curious and deserve to be recalled. I borrow the details as well as the quotations below from the sympathetic brochure published by Charles Edouard Guillaume for the Fête du Soleil of June 1912 under the title: "The First Quarter-Century of the Eiffel Tower."

Seven thousand tons of steel were used, seven million kilograms. To prove its sage economy, one may suppose the tower reduced to thirty centimeters in height while preserving the same relationship of its weight to its size. It would then weigh seven grams, as heavy as a sheet of letter-paper. A cylinder as high as the tower and whose base would embrace its four feet would contain a volume of air whose weight would exceed that of the steel used. The mass of iron, reduced to a uniform sheet covering the square of the base, 125 meters on a side, would be no more than six centimeters thick. These verifications, which make for a kind of game, nonetheless demonstrate an engineering virtuosity, a knowledge of the use of materials of which otherwise it would be difficult to get an idea.

Now what shall we say of the absurd predictions which accompanied the building of Eiffel's project? During the two years of construction, it was rarely spared. One would never see the tower finished, the wind would bend it, lightning would smash or melt it, changes of temperature twist it. Catastrophe was assured, foreseen, desired. Construction did not take two full years and was completed without accidents, or surprises, by dint of the technique itself. Attacked by winds, the courageous Tower was content to describe small ellipses of ten to twelve centimeters. Struck by lightning, it sang like a tuning-fork. On dog-days, the heat on one side caused it to make a slight bow of several centimeters, but there was no catastrophe.

Living its strange life, animated by an imperceptible oscillation, erect beneath the sun, withdrawn when the sky is gray, glorious and resonant, the Tower has resisted both man and the elements. Today the Tower is indispensable, essential to us, and we no longer need statistical records to admire it.

For beyond its ingenious conception, this masterpiece of mathematical genius had its origins in the subconscious realm of beauty. It is more than a figure or a number since it contains a kind of profound vitality which our minds must accept if we look for feeling in the arts of sculpture and architecture.

I would like to offer the most striking yet at the same time simplest example: a plumb-line, motionless, suspended in the center of a free space.

It is the purest element of sculptural language about which man has a certain, indispensable, inexplicable idea. This harmony, absolute and concrete, makes a point of infinity tangible for man. And it is because he has translated this basic truth, without cluttering it, that Eiffel has created a lasting, living work.

For us, now, the cycle of iron is closed; but the chain of human effort is richer by one more link. After fifty years we are proud to bring to it the homage of our younger generation, in gratitude for a lesson of energy and power with which our artistic dreams of today are filled.

The masters of today, who do not fear that the heavens will fall in on them, will be able to show that a new hour is sounding to those masters who announced and prepared the future.

I think that we must state to whom we owe this hour.

Raymond Duchamp-Villon

Letter to John Quinn

[Published by permission of the New York Public Library.]

John Quinn was Duchamp-Villon's largest single collector, and, by the time of the sculptor's death in 1918, owned sixteen works. He bought the first piece, *Girl of the Wood*, 1911, from the Armory Show in 1913, undoubtedly at the suggestion of Walter Pach who had brought the work to America, and who more than any other person was responsible for Duchamp-Villon's reputation here. Among the works purchased by Quinn was *Seated Woman* of 1914, and the preparatory drawing, mentioned here (both now Museum of Art, Rhode Island School of Design). Duchamp-Villon had sent a plaster from which Quinn had a bronze cast (no. 23) made in New York with the artist's knowledge.

What is most interesting, however, is the poignant description of the despair Duchamp-Villon felt at his enforced severance from the intellectual life of which he had been so vital a part in prewar Paris.

The whereabouts of the original letter is unknown, and the text exists only in the awkward translation printed here.

With the armies.
April 8, 1916

Dear Monsieur,

I have to apologize for not having answered you since so long a time. You know how little we are ourselves for the present, and you cannot imagine the effort necessary to evade by the mind, even for a moment, the world of the war. In fact, it is a world, really, which is complete in itself, in its ways and in its ends.

For what counts the thought of one man in this whirlwind, and, above all, what is that thought able to do? We are as far away from Paris, where some friends are working now, as from New York. Any connection between intellectual life and us is broken, and for an undetermined time.

Then, that is why I shall leave in silence the little work I succeeded in accomplishing in lost hours, and which shall be used later when, at last, it will be possible to think about realizations.

Perhaps this rest forced upon our artistic faculties will be a benefit. I know already, now, I have a clearer and surer vision of the road passed over and of the road to go over. And it is restful to see that, without being satisfied in anything, I have nevertheless nothing to regret.

Only, the conditions in which we are going to find ourselves on the morrow of the peace, in a Europe mentally and financially rebuilding, are a little disquieting. But there are enough clouds in our sky not to dream of those which will come later.

So, I will leave this subject to thank you for sending me the cast of the "Woman Seated," which arrived at its destination with a few breaks, but now repaired. Your so gracious attention gave me much pleasure. Be sure that the conventions concerning that sculpture will be respected just as well as those concerning the other works you possess. I also received your letter containing the draft, which ends definitely your acquisitions of my sculptures.

I hope, without playing the prophet, this year will see me in New York, and that I will have the very great satisfaction of knowing you, and, at the same time, have the pleasure of seeing over there all our friends. But . . . of what doesn't one dream?

Very cordially yours,

Raymond Duchamp-Villon

Kinds of Awareness in Artistic Creation (from an unfinished manuscript)

(Variations de la connaisance pendant le travail d'art)

In late 1916 Duchamp-Villon contracted typhoid fever while stationed at the front. He was confined to a hospital for almost two years, his strength slowly fading, before he died. During this agonizing and literally horrible period, he was able to do only one sculpture, the small head of *Professor Gosset*. To maintain contact with intellectual life, the only reality he knew, Duchamp-Villon drafted this manuscript as an articulation of the creative process and the emergence of a work of art. In some respects it is a curious document, eclectic in its sources, which range from Symbolist aesthetics to Bergson, and badly written in parts. It is nevertheless an eloquent statement, bearing testimony to the utter dedication he had given his art and his uncompromising search for the most profound states of consciousness known to the artist.

An artist's constant concern is to know one object or several, and we must designate as an artist even a man who has not yet created anything at all, in order to avoid confusion with similar preoccupations in other professions. He who will become an artist already is one, and within himself the desire to work exists potentially, as well as the means of realizing it. The same elective affinities that lead him to find in objects his sole satisfaction for living will later bring him the imperious satisfaction of escaping from himself by giving of himself. If it were otherwise we would have to understand how one kind of person could be transformed into another person of a different psychic make-up, at what period and at what moment such a transformation would occur, and what cause could provoke it—an arbitrary conception, in conflict with a search for perfection. Besides, an artist's life is nothing more than a search for perfection.

The need to know objects and to bring them to life occurs, then, for the gifted individual before any need to exteriorize. This stage is not without significance and entails a judgement and a choice whose reasons are neither reasoned nor reasonable. Instinctive? Perhaps. Intuitive? Doubtless, but more certainly effective. The artist who is attracted by or simply interested in an object attaches importance to that object only if

BROTHERS WHO PAINT THOSE QUEER CUBIST PICTURES

In the Photograph These Three Creators of "Advanced Art" Seem Quite Normal, and New Yorkers Who Know the French Cubists Assert That Outside of Their Studios They Look and Act Not Differently from Other Men.
Left to Right—Marcell Duchamp, Painter of "Nude Descending a Staircase"; Jacques Villon, Whose Picture "Girl at the Piano" Was Also Shown Here, and Raymond Duchamp-Villon, the Cubist Sculptor. All Three Were Exhibitors at the Recent International Art Show in the Sixty-ninth Regiment Armory.

Marcel Duchamp, Jacques Villon and Raymond Duchamp-Villon and their dog Pipp, photographed in Puteaux in the winter of 1913

he takes possession of it to the extent of identifying himself with it. There is, at the beginning, a display of instinct or intuition, then an affective desire that assures the fusion of thought with the object thought about. This is the necessary condition for all creative activity of which the object will be the pretext.

An emotion is born, it develops under various influences almost to the point of maturity which will permit its realization. At the very beginning there is a simple satisfaction, the fact of having acquired for thought by means of thought a series of phenomena, and having enriched the self with them—a satisfaction that is quickly exhausted, although it may be nourished for a while by the joy of experiencing it before anyone else. At this point one risks having the feeling fade away, and this is frequently the case if some stronger feeling comes into being. It is interesting to note, by the way, that on this score it is not a matter of one image effacing another and that these emotional acquisitions persist, whether they remain in the center of consciousness or not. At the beginning of an artist's development this task of incorporating some outside life, accord-

121

ing to the choice imposed on him by his taste for pleasure, is very intense and, without his suspecting it, this task prepares the way for the various stages which will mark the artist's career.

The accusation that imaginative persons are lazy during their youth is thus easily explained. And it can't be otherwise. What ordinary education offers them has only a remote usefulness, and often hampers the necessary development of their imperiously individual faculties.

At that time the behavior of these young artists can be justified only by their hesitant efforts to create, and, for that reason, they deserve the sarcasm they receive. This state of being, their youth, will for a long time continue to characterize the best of them whose work, becoming more strenuous day by day, is accomplished slowly. Their fate would be unbearable if it were not so beautiful. In the hodge-podge of effective images avidly acquired over an indeterminate time, there are certain ones which often recur and demand attention with an insistence that can become obsessive. When emotion, like a ripe fruit, can no longer remain attached to the tree that bears it, then the need for exteriorization begins: the work of art will take its turn at coming to life, it will inscribe its curve in time, and the creator will want to believe that this curve is going to be as long as possible. He cannot think otherwise since at this time he is mustering all the powers of his being and all its infinite possibilities, and with each new effort he rejects what caused his past frustrations.

The work to be realized is, in some ways, a sort of meeting ground, a reciprocal penetration of the outside world and the Self.[1] What mechanism presides over its creation? Is it a question of modes that vary with the individual? In what way is the creation of art different from all that is created by thought?

Agitation, sadness, then calm, a return to work, uneasiness, short, intermittent attempts to carry on the task, until the moment when a chance movement brings out a point, a line, a color, a volume, or, more often, a note that one had already grasped and thought through during the period of gestation. Most often, it is a matter of an earlier idea that is rediscovered by chance. The memory of the cruel period is abruptly effaced, so that before a space opening before him and which is filled with promise, the artist grows dizzy and trembles with anxiety . . . The joy he has waited for so long is there, he is going to attain it.

The cycle closes, the first feeling is reconstructed in the work that is coming to an end. The sketch grows larger and dominates everything. Certainty has returned. One must insist on this period, marked by anxiety, born in uneasy and painful obscurity; fumblingly, it gathers its scattered forces, weaves their strands into the cord with which the bow will be re-strung.

It has no relation to the period of effort which precedes it, a period whose extent and violence varies with each attempt, from the worst pain to the most tranquil development.

1. It can no longer be just the object, it can no longer be just the Self, it must be a creation.

122

It is a function of the individual himself; and the state which provokes it is always registered at the same moment, when the creative mechanism is functioning, in a perceptibly constant length of time. This is a prelude that the creator recognizes and by which he will accurately judge the rest of the work.

We shall see that there is nothing exceptional about this stage of the creative feeling, and that one always finds something like this when a human being is in the presence of a new state of equilibrium. This is one of the most important observations to make if one is to define that lever of all activity, an emotion—whether creative or not. From this point of view, seekers after perfection permit themselves more typical observations, by addressing themselves to the same phenomena during their very varied labors. With a maximum show of energy they pass through the affective stages which are lighted with an intensity that makes them easy to study. The artist has lifted a corner of the veil, he is worried, he knows that the image in his mind is superimposed on the image he is constructing. The joy which he has hitherto repressed, increases; all the possibilities of the work appear to him, and he sees so many of them that the work, as it is, no longer satisfies him. His knowledge has broadened and he is already looking among his affective riches, acquired during his random pleasures, for the image that will permit him to develop it. And while in the course of finishing the work, he already begins the following one, sometimes only in his mind, sometimes by sketching it. This is the moment that marks the peak of the emotional curve, the point at which there is the intense joy of an intermediate state dominating the past in the finished work and at the same time soaring over the future through the work that will be done tomorrow. A dizzy flight whose shadow gently touches the rugged ground of his labors, the ground of his hopes, whence he comes and whither he'll return. Twilight and dawn, radiant penumbra, calm bewilderment; such contradictions meet and unite, and everything takes on an appearance of probable truth. All is harmony. The human being is, for an instant, in a *state of equilibrium.*

The life of an imaginative person is no more than a series of newly articulated states of consciousness, linked by these transient flights whose curve progresses with the imagination's increasing power and then declines until its death. His work can be judged only as a whole since it represents the entire development of the Self, as projected, and since there can be no break in it. This linking together of successive works of art is inevitable; they complete themselves by giving birth to each other, and no one can predict how they will appear. The artist, at each flight, becomes conscious of this, but he can only store up in his memory aspects that are non-temporal and spacially unuseable. On the contrary, his original feelings, like seeds to be cultivated, keep fresh in his memory and he often draws on those reserves. Long neglected, even the first of all will necessarily revive when he is old and weary, and new ideas occur at longer intervals so that they are costlier and rarer. X . . . was right when he said that at twenty one is one's whole life, abridged.

In the plastic arts it is interesting to note the familiar allegory of the winged figure which allows the artist easily to obtain for himself and his work that state of equilibrium he instinctively desires. In all schools of art pretexts for escaping the laws of gravity are numerous and varied and, like the rest, have been legitimized, catalogued, codified—quite uselessly. The repetition of the means chosen for attaining a maximum intensity of emotion in the creator and the spectator alike is found in all religious art, literary or plastic. This is something to study and will be developed later: it permits us, however, to discover right now the intimate relation between an emotion and the means that produced it. The one begins as soon as the other appears. If every man cannot call himself an exceptional artist, then the exceptional one cannot be just any artist at all. A choice of means forces itself upon him for a number of reasons as we shall see, and the best artist is the one who resists temptation by any of the means used by the other arts.

Nevertheless, in a given group, there is no rule for defining in advance just who is going to be the painter, the sculptor, the musician or the poet. Each of them is made up of analogous qualities, with a predominance of one or another of these qualities, according to the individual. It is evident that a good physique and strong muscles entail a desire to tackle hard matter, with all the slow patient willpower such a task involves. That is the *raison d'être* of a sculptor. However, this enforced slowness cannot make one forget one's original feelings, and it requires of the artist a constancy protected from distractions, and even a bit solemn. The need not to lose one's foothold involves a taste for the physical qualities of matter. Notions of volume, coherence, hardness, weight and even duration accompany the most constructive ideas of space and the relation between spaces—for, in the light of pure speculation, volumes take on a special life and lose all consistency, which is the reason for the small importance lent, at the beginning of a conception, to the material that will be chosen. One could almost say that the sculptor, bit by bit, brings his immaterial creation down to the point where it is crystallized in matter. It is really a question of creation, and couldn't one say that this is more like a translation? The choice of means, different for the sculptor and for the painter, would seem to indicate a need to adopt a language for each form of art, a language that each person will modify according to his own law.

The painter replaces vision in volume by colored vision, and the relation of volumes to each other by a value mechanism. He has, over the sculptor, the advantage of realizing his conception more rapidly, and his imagination gains accordingly in sharpness and suppleness, his language is more easily understood, more alive by virtue of its sensorial action, accessible to the general public. All of which does not mean that it is necessary to deduce the superiority of one or the other of these means of expression. Nor that it is necessary to grant a private language only to them, since all activity straining for perfection has to adopt a new language and since every material object is capable of being perfected.

It is customary to distinguish between the work of art and other objects, created by man's ingenuity for man's use. Therein lies the origin of a misunderstanding which, because of a false classification, retards the public's education in the use of its sensitivity. What minimal limits can one assign to beauty? The best results are known to us, but at what moment does the least good cease to be good at all? Can one say that an object is perfectly beautiful? We admit that perfect beauty cannot exist. Why can't one say that an object is perfectly ugly? People's ideas on this subject are infinitely varied and the apparent unanimity of opinion about certain works is imposed by time and tradition. Rare are those for whom the choice is personal, and even they know only too well how susceptible to change is their taste, and to what an extent it remains a function of the education they are progressively acquiring. The notion of the beautiful cannot be defined in certain objects and excluded from others; it is everywhere, in different degrees, differently perceived in its extreme manifestations. That is verifiable in all forms of art, literature. . . .

(end of manuscript)

["**Opinions**" (au Salon d'Automne), *Montjoie!* v. 1, no. 11–12 (November–December 1913), p. 14.]

Despite its brevity, this statement, concerning the sculpture at the Salon, contains the very essence of Duchamp-Villon's sculptural approach.

Unfortunately nearly all of it is in the domain of modeling, which is quite far from that of sculpture.

Chronology

Raymond Duchamp-Villon and Jacques
Villon in uniforms of the Lycée Corneille
at Rouen

1876 Born Pierre-Maurice-Raymond Duchamp, November 5, Damville (Eure) near Rouen, the second of six children; his father a lawyer and notary; his maternal grandfather Emile-Frederick Nicolle, an accomplished engraver, from whom Duchamp-Villon may have received his first artistic training.

1894 Completed his studies at the Lycée Corneille, Rouen; entered the Université de Paris as a medical student.

1898 Shortly before completion of his medical studies, suffered a severe attack of rheumatic fever, which forced him to abandon his studies.

**1899–ul
1900** Made tentative informal efforts at modeling while a medical student; during long convalescence became absorbed with sculpture and decided to devote himself to it.

c. 1901 Changed name to Duchamp-Villon at father's insistence; settled in Paris at 9, rue Campagne-Première.

1902	First exhibited, Salon de la Société Nationale des Beaux-Arts.
1903	Married, moved to Neuilly-sur-Seine; exhibited for second time at Société Nationale des Beaux-Arts.
1905	First exhibited at Salon d'Automne, where he showed annually until 1913; exhibited at Galerie Legrip, Rouen, with Jacques Villon.
1907	Appointed to jury of the sculpture section, Salon d'Automne; moved to Puteaux with Villon, and later Kupka, in adjoining studios.
1910	Appointed vice-president of jury, Salon d'Automne.
1911	Instrumental in placing of Cubists as a group in Salle VII, Salon d'Automne; began regular Sunday meetings at Puteaux with his brothers, Gleizes, Metzinger, Léger, La Fauconnier, Gris, de la Fresnaye, Lhote, Picabia, Delaunay, Archipenko, Mare, as well as writers and critics Apollinaire, Roger Allard, André Salmon and Alexandre Mercereau. Group also met regularly at Gleizes' studio at Courbevoie on Mondays.
1911	November, exhibited at Galerie de l'Art Contemporain.
1912	October, included in famous Section d'Or exhibition, Paris, Galerie La Boétié. November, joined group, "Artistes de Passy," founded by Henri-Martin Barzun, editor of modern review *Poème et Drame*. Group centered around Puteaux artists, held monthly dinners.
1913	February, exhibited at Armory Show. April, exhibited at Galerie Groult, with Villon, Gleizes and Metzinger. September, with Gleizes helped to organize French section of the Erster Deutscher Herbstsalon, Berlin.
1914	February–March, exhibited Manés Society, Prague, with Gleizes, etc. June–July, exhibited with Gleizes, Metzinger and Villon at the Der Sturm Gallery, Berlin. August, two weeks after war was declared, enlisted as a medical underofficer, 11th Regiment of Cuirassiers; stationed at hospital, St. Germain, and was able to return to Puteaux on frequent leaves to finish his major work, *Le Cheval*.
1915	September, transferred to front.
1916	Stationed at Champagne; in late November or early December contracted typhoid fever, removed to hospital at Mourmelon.
1917	Condition worsened, slowly lost strength.
1918	October 7—died, Cannes Military Hospital.
1919	Retrospective exhibition, Salon d'Automne.
1926	Retrospective exhibition, Salon des Indépendants.

Bibliography

by Bernard Karpel

Librarian, Museum of Modern Art, New York

The compiler wishes to acknowledge, with appreciation, the availability of documentation on Duchamp-Villon previously reported by Mlle. Chantal Maisonnier.

Writings by the Artist

L'architecture et le fer. *Poème et Drame* v. 7, pp. 22–29, March 1914. Reprinted below.

L'architecture et le fer. *Werk* v. 51, pp. 157–158, April 1964. "Texte original d'un article qui parut il y a cinquante ans dans un périodique parisien."

Écrits de Raymond Duchamp-Villon. *In* Galerie Louis Carré. Duchamp-Villon: Le Cheval Majeur. Paris, 1966. pp. 30–39.

(Letters to Walter Pach) (Paris—New York, 1914 ff). Quoted in Knoedler Co. monograph (1967). Copies in files of Museum of Modern Art Library as follows: *1914* (March 17; May 14; July 14; July 20)—*1917* (January 17)—*1919* (August 10). Manuscripts in Pach estate.

Opinions (au Salon d'Automne). *Montjoie!* v. 1, no. 11–12, p. 14, November–December 1913. Illustrated by "Les Amants."

Project d'article sur le Salon d'Automne de 1911. *In* Galerie Louis Carré. Duchamp-Villon: Le Cheval Majeur. Paris, 1966. pp. 32–33. Previously unpublished text.

Réponse à une enquête au sujet de *La Danse* de Carpeaux à l'Opéra. *Gil Blas*, September 17, 1912. Reprinted below.

Réponse à une enquête au sujet de *La Danse* de Carpeaux à l'Opéra. *In* Galerie Louis Carré. Duchamp-Villon; Le Cheval Majeur. Paris, 1966. pp. 30–32.

La Tour Eiffel. *In* Galerie Louis Carré. Duchamp-Villon: Le Cheval Majeur. Paris, 1966. pp. 34–39.

Variations de la connaissance pendant le travail de l'art. *In* Walter Pach. Raymond Duchamp-Villon. Paris, Povolozky, 1924. pp. 29, 32–33. Extracts also below (1954). Manuscript in Walter Pach estate.

Variations de la connaissance pendant le travail de l'art. *In* Begründer der modernen Plastik. Zurich, Kunsthaus Zurich, November 27–December 1954. pp. 6–7.

Additional materials include: Unpublished manuscript notes in the Villon estate (undated, probably 1911)—Letter to John Quinn, April 8, 1916 (New York Public Library)—Unpublished memoir by Mrs. André Roosevelt: "Stories and anecdotes about some early Cubists," with references to Duchamp-Villon and others.

Works on the Artist

PACH WALTER. A Sculptor's Architecture. New York, Association of American Painters and Sculptors, 1913. 21 pp. Booklet for distribution at the famous "Armory Show."

PACH, WALTER. Raymond Duchamp-Villon, Sculpture 1876–1918. Imprimé pour John Quinn et ses Amis. Paris, Jacques Povolozky Éditeur, 1924. 87 pp., 26 ill., port. Includes extracts from letters and original manuscripts. Text also published in English in Guggenheim Museum "Three Brothers" show, New York, 1957.

HAMILTON, GEORGE HEARD and AGEE, WILLIAM C. Raymond Duchamp-Villon. New York, Walker and Co., 1967. 141 pp., 82 ill. Issued on the occasion of a major retrospective at the Knoedler Gallery. Includes quotations from the artist's writings, oeuvre catalog, bibliography. Hamilton text also published in *L'Oeil*, September 1967.

General Works

APOLLINAIRE, GUILIAUME. Chroniques d'Art (1902–1918). Paris, Gallimard, 1960. pp. 200, 202, 281, 342–343, 345, 380, 405–406.

Full Duchamp-Villon references by Apollinaire should include: *L'Intransigeant* (October 11, 14, 1911; November 19, 29, 1913)—*Paris Journal* (May 19, July 3, 1914)—*Soirées de Paris* (November 15, 1913; November 15, 1914).

APOLLINAIRE, GUILLAUME. Les Peintres cubistes. Méditations esthétiques. Paris, Figuière, 1913. pp. 73 ff; pl. 37–41.

> Several printings and later editions, e.g., Athéna, 1922, also 1950, 1962.

APOLLINAIRE, GUILLAUME. Les Peintres cubistes. Méditations esthétiques. Geneva, Cailler, 1950. pp. 79–82; pl. 42–45.

APOLLINAIRE, GUILLAUME. The Cubist Painters. Aesthetic Meditations 1913. New York, Wittenborn, 1962 (c. 1949).

> "Appendix: Duchamp-Villon," pp. 48–50. General bibliography on the writer and Cubism by B. Karpel. Illustrations not those of the original edition.

AZCOAGA, ENRIQUE. El Cubismo. Barcelona, Omega, 1949. p. 22; pl. 45.

BARR, ALFRED H., JR. Cubism and Abstract Art. New York, Museum of Modern Art, 1936. pp. 103–116, 208–209, 243–244; ill.

> Includes exhibition catalog. Reprint issued 1966 by the Museum and Arno Press, N.Y.

BASLER, ADOLPHE. La Sculpture moderne en France. Paris, Crès, 1928. Illustration, pl. 19.

BENEZIT, E. Dictionnaire des Peintres, Sculpteurs; Dessinateurs et Graveurs. Paris, Grund, 1950. Vol. 3, p. 365.

BENOIST, LUC. La Sculpture française. Paris, Presses Universitaires de France, 1963. Illustration, p. 170.

BROWN, MILTON W. American Painting from the Armory Show to the Depression. Princeton, N.J., Princeton University Press, 1955. pp. 49, 113.

BROWN, MILTON W. The Story of the Armory Show. (New York) Joseph H. Hirshhorn Foundation (distributed by the New York Graphic Society), 1963. Pp. 48, 69, 97, 99, 104, 108, 240–241; 1 ill.

> Nos. 609–613 (with notes). Catalogue of Armory Show (*revised*), p. 217 ff.

CABANNE, PIERRE. L'Épopée du Cubisme. Paris, La Table Ronde, 1963. 1 ill.

CAMFIELD, WILLIAM A. "La Section d'Or". New Haven, Yale University, 1961. Pp. 42–44.

> Master's thesis in typescript. Includes Xerox copy of 1912 catalog. General bibliography.

CASSOU, JEAN. Panorama des Arts plastiques contemporaines. Paris, Gallimard, 1960. pp. 204–206, 213, 248, 250, 261, 291–292, 295 (chronology), 420, 592; ill. (p. 264).

CASSOU, JEAN and OTHERS. Gateway to the Twentieth Century. New York, London, McGraw-Hill, 1962. pp. 64, 107, 136, 140, 141–143, 155; 1 ill.

CHENEY, SHELDON. A Primer of Modern Art. New York, Boni & Liveright, 1927. pp. 305–310; 2 ill.

> Many editions, e.g., New York, Tudor, 1939 (10th revised).

CIRLOT, JUAN EDUARDO. La Escultura del Siglo XX. Barcelona, Omega, 1956. pp. 31–32; pl. 28.

COLOMBIER, PIERRE du and MANUEL, ROLAND. Les Arts. Paris, Éditions du XXe Siècle (1933?). p. 161.

COQUIOT, GUSTAVE. Cubistes, Futuristes, Passéistes. Essai sur la jeune Peinture et la jeune Sculpture. Paris, Ollendorf, 1914. Second ed., 1923.

COQUIOT, GUSTAVE. Les Indépendants (1884–1920). Paris, Ollendorf, 1920.

COURTHION, PIERRE. L'Art indépendant. Paris, Michel, 1958. pp. 100, 192, 266, 272; 1 ill.

DELEVOY, ROBERT L. Dimensions of the 20th Century. Geneva, Skira, 1965. pp. 138, 140 (col. plate).

DICTIONNAIRE DE LA SCULPTURE MODERNE. Paris, Hazen, 1960. pp. 83–85; 3 ill.

> Text by J.-E. Muller. Also English edition: *Dictionary of Modern Sculpture*. Edited by Robert Maillard, New York, Tudor, 1960.

DREIER, KATHERINE S. Modern Art, New York, Société Anonyme, 1926. p. 20 (port., 1 ill.).

> On cover: International Exhibition of Modern Art arranged by the Société Anonyme for the Brooklyn Museum, November–December 1926.

EINSTEIN, CARL. Die Kunst des 20. Jahrhunderts. Berlin, Propylaen, 1931. pp. 218, 227, 592, 648; 1 ill.

EDOUARD-JOSEPH, RENÉ. Dictionnaire biographique des Artistes contemporains, 1910–1930. Paris, Art & Édition, 1930, and Grund, 1934. Vol. I, p. 431 (1930)—III, pp. 395–396, 3 ill. (1934).

FAURE, ELIE. History of Art, Vol. 4: Modern Art. New York, Harper, 1924. p. 500.

> Translated from the French. Also: Oeuvres complètes. Paris, Pauvert, 1964. Vol. II, p. 252.

FRANCASTEL, PIERRE, ed. Les Sculpteurs célèbres. Paris, Mazenod, 1954. pp. 306–307, port.

Text by Jacques Villon.

FRY, EDWARD F. Cubism. London, Thames & Hudson, 1966. pp. 61, 93, 111, 119, 132, 136, 173, 175.

Includes extracts from contemporaneous reviews and essays, 1905–44, e.g., Raynal, *The Section d'Or exhibition 1912*, pp. 97–110. Also continental editions.

GERTZ, ULRICH. Contemporary Plastic Art, 2nd enl. ed. Berlin, Rembrandt, 1955. pp. iv–v, 256; pl. 128.

GIEDION-WELCKER, CAROLA. Moderne Plastik. Zurich, Girsberger, 1937.

Translation: Modern Plastic Art, 1937. Enlarged Wittenborn edition, 1955.

GIEDION-WELCKER, CAROLA. Contemporary Sculpture, an Evolution in Volume and Space. New York, Wittenborn, 1955. Pp. xiii, 20, 68, 73, 263 (port.), 265–266 (biography), 307 (bibliography), 7 ill.

Also published by Faber & Faber (London), and by Verlag Hatje (Stuttgart) as: Plastik des XX. Jahrhunderts.

GINISTRY, P. Les Artistes morts pour la Patrie. Paris, 1916 and 1919. pp. 59–61.

GISCHIA, L. and VÉDRÈS, N. La Sculpture en France depuis Rodin. Paris, Éditions du Seuil, 1945. Pl. 1–3.

GLEIZES, ALBERT. Du Cubisme et des Moyens de la comprendre. Paris, La Cible, 1920.

Reproduces "Le Cheval" (plaster). For contemporaneous theory see his 1912 text, or the English translation: *Cubism*, by Albert Gleizes and Jean Metzinger. London, Unwin, 1913.

GOLDING, JOHN. Cubism: a History and Analysis, 1907–1914. New York, Wittenborn, 1959. Also translation: *Le Cubisme*. Paris, Juillard, 1962. pp. 154–156; fig. 71.

GRAY, CHRISTOPHER. Cubist Aesthetic Theories. Baltimore, John Hopkins Press, 1953. 190 pp.

Bibliography, pp. 171–181. While Gray omits any reference to Duchamp-Villon, he presents the critical and philosophical aspects of the movement in detail.

GREGG, FREDERICK J., ed. For and Against: Views on the International Exhibition held in New York and Chicago. New York, Association of American Painters and Sculptors, 1913.

Includes "The Cubist Room" by Walter Pach, pp. 51–55.

HOFMANN, WERNER. Die Plastik des 20. Jahrhunderts. Frankfurt, Fischer, 1958. pp. 99, 108–109, 114, 156; pl. 15.

JANSON, HORST W. History of Art. New York, Abrams, 1963. P. 534 (ill.).

Also foreign language editions.

JOURDAIN, FRANTZ. Le Salon d'Automne rev. ed. Paris, Les Arts et le Livre, 1928.

Reviews salons from 1908–1925.

KUHN, WALT. The Story of the Armory Show. New York, the Author, 1938. pp. 11, 26.

LICHT, FRED. Sculpture 19th & 20th Centuries. Greenwich, Conn., New York Graphic Society; London, Rainbird, 1967. pp. 331, 333; 2 ill.

LYNTON, NORBERT. The Modern World. New York, Toronto, McGraw-Hill, 1965. pp. 47, 64, 101, 103–104, 107, 163; 2 ill.

"Landmarks of the World's Art" series.

MCCURDY, CHARLES, ed. Modern Art: A Pictorial Anthology. New York, Macmillan, 1958. pp. 231–232; 2 ill.

MARCHIORI, GIUSEPPE. Modern French Sculpture. New York, Abrams, 1963. pp. 25–27; pl. xxv, xxvi (color).

OZENFANT, AMÉDÉE. Art. Paris, Budry, 1928. Chap. IV.

Revised 1929. German edition: Leben und Gestaltung (Potsdam, 1931), p. 58. English and American editions (1931); revised American edition, 1952.

PACH, WALTER. The Masters of Modern Art. New York, Huebsch, 1924. Pp. 85–86, 111–112; pl. 28–29.

Comments on "Baudelaire" and "The Horse."

PACH, WALTER. Queer Thing, Painting. Forty Years in the World of Art. New York, Harper, 1938. pp. 137, 218, 220–221, 226; port., 1 ill.

Chap. XI: The Three Brothers. Also brief note in his: *Ananias or the False Artist*. New York, Harper, 1928. p. 231.

PLATTE, HANS. Plastik. Munich, Piper, 1957. Pp. 82–84, 290, 298; 1 ill.

PRADEL, MARIE-NOËLLE. Raymond Duchamp-Villon: la Vie et l'Oeuvre. Paris, 1960.

"Thèse soutenue à l'École du Louvre, 9 janvier."

READ, HERBERT. A Concise History of Modern Sculpture. New York, Praeger, 1964. p. 291; pl. 72, 74, 119.

RITCHIE, ANDREW C. Sculpture of the Twentieth Century. New York, Museum of Modern Art, 1952. Pp. 27–38, 136–137, 227; 2 ill.

ROSENBLUM, ROBERT. Cubism and Twentieth-

Century Art. New York, Abrams, 1961. pp. 152, 263–264, 266; pl. 191, 193, 194.

Chap. IV: Cubism and twentieth-century sculpture. General chronology and bibliography.

SALMON, ANDRÉ. La Jeune Sculpture française. Paris, Société des Trente (Messein), 1919. p. 92.

Complemented by series "La sculpture vivant," *L'Art Vivant*, 1926 (pp. 140–141, 208–211, 258–260, 334–335, 743–744; ill.).

SCHLENOFF, NORMAN. Art in the Modern World. New York, Toronto, Bantam, 1965. p. 187.

SELZ, JEAN. Modern Sculpture: Origin and Evolution. New York, Braziller, 1963. pp. 212, 219, 222, 238; pl. 196–198, XII.

SÉRULLAZ, MAURICE. Le Cubisme. Paris, Presses Universitaires de France, 1963. p. 107.

SEUPHOR, MICHEL, ed. L'Art abstrait: ses Origines, ses premiers Maîtres. Paris, Maeght, 1949.

SEUPHOR, MICHEL. The Sculpture of This Century. New York, Braziller, 1960. pp. 29–31, 260–261, 360; 2 ill.

Translation from: La Sculpture de ce Siècle. Neuchâtel, Griffon, 1959.

THIEME, U. and BECKER, F., ed. Allgemeines Lexikon der bildenden Künstler. Leipzig, Seemann, 1913. Vol. 10, p. 33.

Does not include references to "literary" periodicals, e.g., *Poème et Drame* v. 6, January 1913 (on "Passy"), September–October 1913 (by H.-M. Barzun)—*Paris Journal*, November 18, 1913 (H. Revers)—*L'Intransigeant*, April 11, 1914 (J. Barreyre).

TRIER, EDUARD. Figur und Raum: die Skulptur des XX. Jahrhunderts. Berlin, Mann, 1960. pp. 39, 72; pl. 102.

TRIER, EDUARD. Moderne Plastik. Frankfurt, Gutenberg, 1955. pp. 43, 86; pl. 41.

VALENTINER, W. R. Origins of Modern Sculpture. New York, Wittenborn, 1946. pp. 61, 70, 132, 172; 2 ill.

Also organized exhibition: Origins of Modern Sculpture. St. Louis City Art Museum, March 30–May 1, 1946. Preface by W. R. Valentiner; no. 99–103 by Duchamp-Villon.

VOLLMER, HANS. Allgemeines Lexikon der bildenden Künstler des XX. Jahrhunderts. Leipzig, Seemann, 1953. Vol. 1, pp. 599–600.

Brief bibliography, including magazine references.

ZERVOS, CHRISTIAN. Histoire de l'Art contemporain. Paris, Cahiers d'Art, 1938. pp. 297, 301 (ill.).

Collections

AMSTERDAM. STEDELIJK MUSEUM. Aanwinstein acquisities, 1945–1954. Amsterdam, 1954. Ill. (fig. 36).

CHICAGO. ART INSTITUTE OF CHICAGO. 20th Century Art from the Louise and Walter Arensberg Collection. Chicago, October 20–December 18, 1949. pp. 10–11, 28, 68; 1 ill.

Text by K. Kuh and D. C. Rich. Collection now in the Philadelphia Museum of Art.

GEORGE WALTER VINCENT SMITH ART GALLERY. Some New Forms of Beauty, 1909–1939. A Selection of the Collection of the Société Anonyme. Springfield, Mass., November 9–December 17, 1939. pp. 15, 18, 20.

Includes chronology of the Société. Lists Duchamp-Villon "Relief" for "official" catalogue.

GUGGENHEIM, PEGGY. Art of This Century. New York, Art of This Century, 1942. p. 65; ill.

Quotes Duchamp-Villon briefly. Frequently exhibited as an "anthology of non-realistic art" with variant catalogs and checklists, e.g., Venice Biennale (1948), Florence and Milan (1949), Brussels ("Surréalisme & Abstraction") 1950, Zurich ("Moderne Kunst") 1951, etc.

GUGGENHEIM, PEGGY. Mostra di Scultura Contemporanea, presentata da Peggy Guggenheim. Venice (Carlo Ferrari), 1949.

Shown September at the Giardino del Palazzo Venier dei Leoni. Preface by G. Marchiori. *Similarly:* La Collezione Peggy Guggenheim. Venice (Palazzo Venier dei Leoni), n.d. p. 15; pl. 60. Prefaces: Sandberg, Read, Barr. Scheduled for publication: Elena and Nicholas Calas. The Peggy Guggenheim Collection of Modern Art. (New York, Abrams, 1967.)

NEW YORK. MUSEUM OF LIVING ART. A. E. Gallatin Collection. New York, 1936.

Catalogs issued 1930, 1933, 1937. Collection begun 1927; now in the Philadelphia Museum of Art.

NEW YORK. MUSEUM OF MODERN ART. Paintings and Sculpture in the Museum of Modern Art. Edited by Alfred H. Barr, Jr. New York, 1942. p. 38 (ill.) No. 183–184, Duchamp-Villon. Also 1948 edition; p. 306; 2 ill. (pp. 268–269).

Also Museum *Bulletin*, v. 21, no. 1, pp. 3, 5; v. 28, no. 2–4, p. 18. The Museum's "Baudelaire," "The Horse" and "The Lovers" have been included in approximately fifty exhibitions in New York and abroad from 1928–1966, e.g., *Cubism and Abstract Art*, *Art in Our Time*, *Masterworks of the 20th Century* (Tate Gallery), etc.

NEW YORK. MUSEUM OF MODERN ART. Masters of Modern Art. Edited by Alfred H. Barr, Jr. New York, 1954. p. 79 (ill.).

PARIS. MUSÉE NATIONAL D'ART MODERNE. Catalogue Guide du Musée National d'Art Moderne (par) Jean Cassou et Bernard Dorival. Paris, 1947.

No. 17, Duchamp-Villon. *Similarly*: La Sculpture contemporaine au Musée d'Art moderne (par) Agnes Humbert. Paris, Morancé, 1954.

PHILADELPHIA. MUSEUM OF ART. The Louise and Walter Arensburg Collection: 20th Century Section. Philadelphia, 1954.

Essay by Henry Clifford. Pl. 86: Head of a Horse (1914); pl. 87: Prof. Gosset (1917).

QUINN, JOHN. Collection of Paintings, Water Colors, Drawings & Sculpture. Huntington, N.Y., Pidgeon Hill Press, 1926. pp. 27–28, 190–191, 200, 3 ill.

Lists sixteen works. Preface by Forbes Watson. Complemented by: The John Quinn Collection, Paintings and Sculptures of the Moderns. New York, American Art Association, 1927. Sale of February 12; nos. 676–722 by Duchamp-Villon. (A letter by the artist to Quinn, dated April 8, 1916, is in the New York Public Library collection.)

SOLOMON R. GUGGENHEIM MUSEUM. A Handbook to the Solomon R. Guggenheim Collection. New York, 1959. p. 200; pl. 176.

YALE UNIVERSITY. ART GALLERY. Collection of the Société Anonyme: Museum of Modern Art 1920. New Haven, Conn., Associates in Fine Arts, 1950. pp. 3–4, ill.

Note by Marcel Duchamp. Brief quote from Duchamp-Villon, brief bibliography. Trustees: Katherine S. Dreier, Marcel Duchamp. Curator: G. H. Hamilton.

Articles

Albright-Knox Art Gallery annual report: 1946–1965. *Gallery Notes* (Buffalo) v. 29, no. 1, pp. 24, 44, ill., March 1966.

Also *Gallery Notes* v. 11, p. 27, 1946 on "Yvonne" acquisition.

BASLER, ADOLPHE. Die neue Plastik in Frankreich. *Jahrbuch der Jungen Kunst* v. 3, pp. 211–216, 1922.

BLOC, ANDRÉ. La sculpture abstraite en France. *Spazio* v. 3, no. 6, pp. 13–20, December 1951–April 1952.

The Brothers. *Time* (New York) April 8, 1957, pp. 74, 77; 1 ill. (col.).

BUSCHE, FREDDY, and GUÉGUEN, PIERRE. Exposition à Yverdon. *Art d'Aujourd'hui* v. 5, nos. 4–5, pp. 38–43, ill. May–June 1954.

CALAS, NICOLAS. The brothers Duchamp all at once. *Art News* (New York) v. 55, pp. 24–27, 56; ill. February 1957.

CALVESI, MAURIZIO. Il Futurismo e l'avanguardia europea. *La Biennale di Venezia* no. 36–37, pp. 21–44, July-Dec. 1959, 1 ill.

CAMFIELD, WILLIAM. Juan Gris and the Golden Section. *Art Bulletin*, pp. 128–134, March 1965. Bibliography.

CLEAVER, DALE. The concept of time in modern sculpture. *Art Journal* v. 22, no. 4, pp. 232–236; ill. Summer 1963.

Bibliography.

COATES, R. M. Duchamp brothers (at the Guggenheim Museum). *New Yorker* v. 33, pp. 99–101, March 2, 1957.

DORIVAL, BERNARD. Raymond Duchamp-Villon au Musée d'Art moderne. *Musées de France* no. 3, pp. 64–68, 3 ill., April 1949.

DORIVAL, BERNARD. Musée National d'Art: six mois d'activité. *La Revue du Louvre* no. 6, pp. 300–306, ill., 1963.

EISENDRATH, W. N. Paintings and sculpture in the collection of Mrs. Mark C. Steinberg. *Connoisseur* v. 154, p. 270, ill., December 1963.

Enquête sur la sculpture. *Cahiers d'Art* v. 3, nos. 9–10 (1928)—v. 4, no. 4 (1929).

ELSEN, ALBERT. The sculpture of Duchamp-Villon. *Artforum*, October 1967. pp. 19 ff.

GIEDION-WELCKER, CAROLA. New roads in modern sculpture. *Transition* no. 23, pp. 198–201, ill., July 1935.

GIEDION-WELCKER, CAROLA. Origines et tendances du relief. *XXe Siècle* no. 21, pp. 3–4, ill., May 1961.

English translation appended.

GIEDION-WELCKER, CAROLA. Verankerung und Vorstoss bei Raymond Duchamp-Villon. *Werk* v. 51, pp. 147–156, 16 ill., April 1964.

GINDERTAËL, R. V. L'époque du Cubisme. *Art d'Aujourd'hui* v. 2, no. 3, pp. 12–13, ill., January 1951.

Special sculpture number.

GINDERTAËL, R. V. L'oeuvre majeure de Duchamp-Villon. *XXe Siècle* no. 23, suppl., pp. (42–44), 4 ill., May 1964.

GREENBERG, CLEMENT. Cross-breeding of modern sculpture. *Art News* v. 51, no. 4, pp. 74–77, 123–124, June–August 1952.

GUÉGUEN, PIERRE. La sculpture cubiste. *Art d'Aujourd'hui* v. 4, nos. 3–4, pp. 53–55, ill., May–June 1953.

Special Cubist number, including "Raymond Duchamp et le cheval mécanique cubiste."

HAMILTON, GEORGE H. Duchamp, Duchamp-Villon, Villon. *Yale Associates Bulletin* v. 13, pp. 1–17, 2 ill., March 1945.

Supplemented by: Duchamp *et al* at Yale University. *Art News* v. 44, p. 9, March 15, 1945.

HAMILTON, GEORGE HEARD. Raymond Duchamp-Villon. *L'Oeil* no. 151–153, pp. 46–56, 82 ill. (ports.), September 1967.

Introduction to Walker and Co. Monograph (New York, 1967).

HAMMACHER, A. M. Raymond Duchamp-Villon (1876–1918) en de beeldhouwkunst Tussen 1910–1914. *Museumjournal (Otterloo)* pp. 4–7, 19, 2 ill., July 1955.

HESS, THOMAS B. Many-sided look at modern sculpture. *Art News* v. 51, no. 6, pp. 16–21, ill., October 1952.

Reviews "Sculpture of the 20th Century."

HOFFMAN, E. (Duchamp family exhibition at the Guggenheim Museum). *Burlington Magazine* v. 99, p. 132, April 1957.

HUNTER, SAM. The Maremont Collection. *Art International* pp. 34–41, ill., July–August 1961.

KAHN, GUSTAVE. La réalisation d'un ensemble d'architecture et de décoration. *L'Art Decoratif* v. 29, pp. 89–102, February 1913.

KAHNWEILER, DANIEL HENRY. Negro art and cubism. *Horizon* no. 108, pp. 412–420, December 1948.

KUH, KATHERINE. Modern sculpture—additions and plans. *Art Institute of Chicago Quarterly* v. 52, pp. 22–23, cover ill., April 1, 1958.

LIEBERMAN, WILLIAM S. Jacques Villon: his graphic art. *Museum of Modern Art Bulletin* v. 21, no. 1, p. 3, Fall 1953.

Cover: "Baudelaire" (Etching, 1921).

MCBRIDE, HENRY. Duchamps du monde (at the Rose Fried Gallery). *Art News* v. 51, pp. 33–35, ill., March 1952.

Similarly reviewed: *Art Digest* v. 26, pp. 16–17, ill., March 15, 1952.

MCMULLEN, R. (Art news from Paris: Duchamp-Villon's "Horse"). *Art News* v. 65, p. 20, September 1966.

MELLQUIST, JEROME. Une famille d'artistes. *Annabelle (Zurich)* pp. 18–19, ill., October 1953.

MICHELSON, ANNETTE. Duchamp-Villon at the Louis Carré gallery. *Art International* v. 7, pp. 87–93, 9 ill., September 25, 1963.

MORRIS, GEORGE L. K. Relations of painting and sculpture. *Partisan Review* no. 1, pp. 63–71, January–February 1943.

NEUGASS, FRITZ. Die Brüder Duchamp-Villon. *Die Weltkunst* p. 5, April 1, 1957.

NEW YORK: La mostra di Jacques Villon, Raymond Duchamp-Villon et Marcel Duchamp. *Emporium* v. 125, pp. 220–223, 1 ill., 1957. Text signed r.f.c.

OESTREICH, DIETER. Formtendenzen unserer Zeit. *Werk* v. 40, no. 6, pp. 194–199, 1953.

PACH, WALTER. Raymond Duchamp-Villon. *Formes* no. 15, pp. 84–85, 2 ill., May 1931.

PAYNE, E. H. Carved relief by Duchamp-Villon. *Detroit Institute Bulletin* v. 26, no. 3, pp. 65–67, 1947.

PRADEL, MARIE-NOËLLE. Dessins de Duchamp-Villon. *La Revue des Arts* nos. 4–5, pp. 221–224, 6 ill., 1960.

PRADEL, MARIE-NOËLLE. La maison cubiste en 1912. *Art de France* no. 1, pp. 176–186, 2 ill., 1961.

RIBEMONT-DESSAIGNES, GEORGES. Avant Dada. *Les Lettres Nouvelles (Paris)* November 1955, pp. 535–548; December 1955, pp. 733–753.

ROSENBLUM, ROBERT. The Duchamp Family. *Arts* v. 31, pp. 20–23, 3 ill., April 1957.

SCHNEIDER, PIERRE. (Sculptures at the Galerie Louis Carré). *Art News* v. 62, p. 17, ill., October 1963.

LA SCULPTURE. *Le Point (Colmar)* v. 2, no. 6, December 1937.

Special number. Essays by Besson, Martinie, Cladel, Roger-Marx.

TAILLANDIER, YVON. "Le Cheval Majeur" de Duchamp-Villon. *Connaissance des Arts* no. 175, p. 19, ill., September 1966.

Similar review in *Aujourd'hui* v. 10, p. 98, September 1966.

TOWNSEND, BENJAMIN. Albright-Knox Gallery, Buffalo: work in progress. *Art News* v. 65, p. 34, ill., January 1967.

VALENTINER, W. R. The simile in sculptural composition. *Art Quarterly* (*Detroit*) v. 10, pp. 262–277, fig. 23, Autumn 1947.

Also *Detroit Institute of Arts Bulletin*, v. 26, pp. 65–67, ill., 1947.

VOLLMER, HANS. Duchamp-Villon. *Allgemeines Lexikon der Bildenden Künstler des XX. Jahrhundert.* v. 1, pp. 599–600, 1953.

Magazine references include: *American Artist* 12:40, ill. (1948)—*Amour de l'Art* 12·337 ff (1931)—*Beaux Arts* 4:98 (1926)—*Chroniques des Arts* 19:157 (1917)—*Cicerone* 21:114 (1929)—Cleveland Museum Bulletin 16:172 (1929), etc.

WATT, ALEXANDER. (Fifteen pieces of sculpture at the Galerie Carré). *Studio* v. 166, p. 122, ill., September 1963.

Similar review in *Aujourd'hui* v. 8, p. 199, ill., October 1963.

WESTHEIM, PAUL. Vom Wesen des plastischen Gestaltens. *Das Kunstblatt* no. 7, pp. 193–208, July 1917.

ZAHN, LEOPOLD. Französische Plastik. *Das Kunstwerk* v. 1, no. 12, pp. 46, 48, ill., 1947–1948.

Similarly *Das Kunstwerk*, no. 1, 1955: Französische Plastik des 20. Jahrhunderts (E. Trier), pp. 35–40, ill.

ZERVOS, CHRISTIAN. Raymond Duchamp-Villon. *Cahiers d'Art* v. 6, no. 4, pp. 226–227, ill., 1931.

ZERVOS, CHRISTIAN. La situation faites au dessin dans l'art contemporain. *Cahiers d'Art* v. 28, p. 161 ff, 1953.

Reproductions include Duchamp-Villon.

Exhibition Catalogs (One-Man and Family)

GROULT, ANDRÉ, GALERIE. Exposition de Sculptures de R. Duchamp-Villon—Aquarelles, Dessins, Pastels d'Albert Gleizes et Jean Metzinger—Gravures de Jacques Villon. Paris, April 6–May 3, 1914.

Illustrates two Duchamp-Villon works.

SALON D'AUTOMNE. Retrospective Raymond Duchamp-Villon. Paris, 1919.

The artist exhibited regularly at the Salon, 1905–1913. Reviewed by Roger Allard, *Nouveau Spectateur* no. 11–12, pp. 20–21, 1919. Other reviews: *Comoedia*, October 20, 1912 (by A. Warnod); *L'Art Décoratif*, November 20, 1912 (by F. Roches); *Les Écrits Français*, November 14, 1913 (by R. Allard).

BRUMMER GALLERY. Memorial Exhibition of the Works of Raymond Duchamp-Villon (1876–1918) New York, January 5–February 9, 1929.

Six-page fold, listing forty-five works and "drawings." Text by Walter Pach.

ARTS CLUB OF CHICAGO. Sculpture by Raymond Duchamp-Villon. March 28–April 12, 1929.

Six-page fold, listing twenty-five works and drawings "loaned by the Brummer Gallery." Preface by Walter Pach.

PIERRE, GALERIE. Sculpture de Duchamp-Villon, 1876–1918. Paris, June 8–27, 1931.

Lists thirty-three works, collectors, brief critiques (1907–1930). Preface by André Salmon ("May 1931"). Five illustrations.

DRU, BOURGEAT ET VAN GELDER, GALERIE. Peintures, gouaches et pastels de Charles Dufresne—Sculptures de Duchamp-Villon. June 10–26, 1931.

Preface by Walter Pach.

FRANCE, GALLERIE DE. Jacques Villon, Peintures de 1909 à 1914—Duchamp-Villon, Sculptures. March 7–20, 1942.

Seven works. Preface by René-Jean.

YALE UNIVERSITY ART GALLERY. Duchamp, Duchamp-Villon, Villon. New Haven, March 1945.

Nos. 25–28 by Duchamp-Villon (2 ill.). Preface by George H. Hamilton. Catalog included in the *Bulletin of the Associates in Fine Arts*, March 1945.

FRIED, ROSE, GALLERY. Duchamp Frères et Soeur. New York, February 25–March 1952.

Four works, one illustration. Preface by Walter Pach.

SOLOMON R. GUGGENHEIM MUSEUM. Jacques Villon—Raymond Duchamp-Villon—Marcel Duchamp. New York, January 8–February 17; Houston, Museum of Fine Arts, March 8–April 8, 1957.

Actually opened February 20 (New York) and March 22 (Houston). Part 3 on Duchamp-Villon (20 pp. incl. ill.). Text by Walter Pach from his 1924 monograph. Excerpts from a letter to Pach (January 16, 1913). Biography. Insert: List of exhibitors (i.e., exhibits): fifteen works, nine illustrations.

CARRÉ, LOUIS, GALERIE. Sculptures de Duchamp-Villon. Paris, 1963. (54) pp. incl. 15 pl., port.

Published on the occasion of the June 17–July 30 show. Text and commentary by Simone Frigerio; documentation by Chantal Maisonnier; photos by Walter Drayer.

CARRÉ, LOUIS, GALERIE. Duchamp-Villon: Le

Cheval Majeur. Paris, June 23–December 24, 1966. (56) pp. incl. ill., port.

Text by Jean Cassou (pp. 7–15), R. V. Gindertaël (pp. 16–20). Photos by Louis Raymond. "Écrits de Raymond Duchamp-Villon" (pp. 30–39). "Choix de textes sur Raymond Duchamp-Villon" (pp. 41–49): Apollinaire, Pach, Salmon, Michelson, Giedion-Welcker.

ROUEN. MUSÉE DE ROUEN. Les Duchamps: Jacques Villon, Raymond Duchamp-Villon, Marcel Duchamp, Suzanne Duchamp. April 15–June 1, 1967.

Fifteen works, fifteen drawings, four illustrations. Preface by Olga Popovitch; biography by Chantal Maisonnier. "Raymond Duchamp-Villon," by Jean Cassou, pp. 57–58.

PARIS. MUSÉE NATIONAL D'ART MODERNE. Raymond Duchamp-Villon, Marcel Duchamp. June 7–July 2, 1967. pp. 1–24 incl. ill.

Preface by Jean Cassou, chronology, lists 30 works, bibliography.

Exhibitions (General)

LA BOÉTIE, GALERIE. Salon de "La Section d'Or." Préface de René Blum. Paris, October 10–30, 1912.

No. 23: "Duchamp-Villon. Sculptures." Another "Exposition de la Section d'Or, 1912–1925" was held by the Galerie Vavin-Raspail, Paris, January 12–31, 1925 (Preface by Guillaume Dalbert).

ASSOCIATION OF AMERICAN PAINTERS AND SCULPTORS, INC. International Exhibition of Modern Art. New York, February 15–March 15, 1913.

Customarily known as the "Armory Show." Nos. 609–613: Architectural Facade—Torso—Fille de Bois—Danseur—Baudelaire (First four in plaster). Also shown at the Art Institute of Chicago, March 24–April 26 (nos. 109–111)—Copley Hall, Copley Society of Boston, April 28–May 18. Exhibition reconstructed 1963.

PHILADELPHIA. MUSEUM OF ART. Sculpture of the Twentieth Century. New York, October 11–December 7, 1952. pp. 16, 42.

Also shown at the Chicago Art Institute

(January 22–March 8), New York Museum of Modern Art (April 29–September 7, 1953). Nos. 27–28: Duchamp-Villon (1 ill.), biographical note. Supplemented by major book by Andrew Ritchie (1952).

PARIS. MUSÉE NATIONAL D'ART MODERNE. Le Cubisme, 1907–1914. January 30–April 9, 1953.

Nos. 34, 86, 118, 164–167, 226 (2 ill.). Preface by Jean Cassou; catalogue by G. Vienne; detailed chronologies.

UTICA, MUNSON-WILLIAMS-PROCTOR INSTITUTE. 1913 Armory Show, 50th Anniversary Exhibition, 1963. February 17–March 31, 1963. pp. 47, 159–160, 179, 188–189.

Duchamp-Villon: no. 609, 610, 611 (3 ill.). Organized by the Institute, sponsored by the Henry St. Settlement, New York. Shown at the Armory of the 69th Regiment, New York, April 6–28. Includes (p. 157ff): Poster (with Duchamp-Villon's name)—W. Kuhn letter to W. Pach, December 12, 1912—"The Cubist room" by W. Pach.

YVERDON. HÔTEL DE VILLE. Sept Pionniers de la Sculpture moderne. Paris, July 18–September 28, 1954.

Nos. 19–23 by Duchamp-Villon (pl. 3–4). Texts by C. Goldscheider, A. H. Barr, Jr., Jacques Villon. Artists' texts edited by M. Seuphor. Exhibit reviewed by C. Giedion Welcker (Werk, September 1954, pp. 209–210).

ZURICH. KUNSTHAUS. Begründer der modernen Plastik. November 27–December 1954.

Nos. 59–68 by Duchamp-Villon (2 ill.); also brief text, chronology, bibliography. (Same show as Yverdon, with addition of Lipchitz).

PARIS. MUSÉE NATIONAL D'ART MODERNE. Les Sources du XXe Siècle. November 4, 1960–January 23, 1961.

Duchamp-Villon: nos. 138–140 (1 ill.) Biographical note, p. 57. Catalogue by A. Chatelet; prefaces by J. Cassou, J. C. Argan, N. Pevsner.

DARTMOUTH COLLEGE. Sculpture in Our Century: Selections from the Joseph H. Hirshhorn Collection. Hanover, N.H., May 25–July 9, 1967.

No. 15: Le Cheval, 1914. Biographical note.

Exhibitions

All exhibitions during Duchamp-Villon's life are included, as well as retrospective and other major exhibitions of his work after his death in 1918. Entries are recorded in full until 1945. Thereafter place and date only are given. Place of exhibition is Paris unless otherwise indicated.

1902

Société Nationale des Beaux Arts. 15 April–30 June.
   67. Portrait de Mme. B——

1903

Société Nationale des Beaux Arts. 15 April–30 June.
   65. Croquis de Catalane

1904

Société Nationale des Beaux Arts. 15 April–30 June.
   1903. Semper eadem (statue plâtre)

1905

Salon d'Automne. 18 October–25 November.
   494. Femme qui lit (marbre)
   495. Joueurs de Foot-Ball (maquette plâtre)
   496. Buste de M. D. (bronze)

Rouen. Galerie Legrip. With Jacques Villon. Date uncertain.

1906

Société Nationale des Beaux Arts. 15 April–30 June.
   1761. Sommeil (étude plâtre)

Salon d'Automne. 6 October–15 November.
   498. Dans le Silence (bronze)
   499. Oesope (buste plâtre)

1907

Salon d'Automne. October 1–22
   501. Torse (étude plâtre)
   502. Vieux Paysan (buste, plâtre)

1908

Société Nationale des Beaux Arts. 15 April–30 June.
   1925. Portrait de femme (plâtre)

Salon d'Automne. 1 October–8 November.
   602. Chanson (groupe plâtre)
   603. Portrait de jeune fille (bronze)

1909

Salon des Indépendants. 25 March–2 May.
   527. Vieux paysan (buste pierre)
   528. Portrait d'enfant (plâtre)

Salon d'Automne. 1 October–8 November.
   461. Jeune fille assise (bronze)
   462. Chanson (bois sculpté)

1910

Salon des Indépendants. 18 March–1 May.
   1585. Portrait d'homme (buste marbre)

Salon d'Automne. 1 October–8 November.
   351. Pastorale (groupe plâtre)

1911

Rouen. Salon de Juin. Société normande de peinture moderne. May–June.
   16. Chanson (sculpture: bois)
   18. Visage d'enfant (terre cuite)

Salon d'Automne. 1 October–8 November.
   403. Nymphe des Bois (bronze)
   404. Baudelaire (buste plâtre)
   405. Vasque décorative (pierre). (Céramique de M. Messoul)

Galerie de l'art ancien et de l'art contemporain. 20 November–16 December. Also included Gleizes, R. de La Fresnaye, Léger, Duchamp, Metzinger, Segonzac, Archipenko.
   10. Baudelaire (buste)

Artistes de Neuilly. Place, date uncertain.
   Chanson; others not identifiable from photos.

1912

Salon d'Automne. 1 October–8 November.
    507. Projet d'hôtel
    Architecture et Sculpture
    Bronzes, terres cuites, sculptures, servant à
    la decoration interieure du même ensemble.

André Mare
    1127. Ensemble composé d'une façade,
    entrée, salon, chambre à coucher, avec la
    collaboration de Duchamp-Villon, J.-L.
    Gampert, Marie Laurencin, R. de la Fres-
    naye, Marie-Thérèse Lanou, Andre Veran,
    M. Marinot, Sabine Desvallières, Richard
    Desvallières, G. Ribemont-Dessaigne,
    Jacques Villon, Paul Vera.
        Sont d'André Mare; les meubles, le papier

peint de l'entrée, le portière et les dessins
de lit, l'etoffe des sièges, les reliures et le
papier à lettres.

_____

Villon, Jacques
    1712. Decoration

Section d'Or, Galerie de la Boétié. October 10–30.
    23. Sculptures

1913

New York. Armory Show. 15 February–15 March.
    Facade for a Residence (plaster)
    Torso (plaster)
    Dancer (plaster)
    Baudelaire
    Fille des Bois (1911), bronze, purchased by
    John Quinn.

Fig. 75   *Kneeling Woman*. Charcoal,
17¼ × 10¹³⁄₁₆ in. Musée National d'Art
Moderne, Paris

Fig. 76   *Kneeling Woman*. Charcoal, 23⅝ × 23⅝ in.
Musée National d'Art Moderne, Paris

137

Fig. 78 *Woman Seated on a Barrel* (verso of fig. 77).
Charcoal

Salon d'Automne. 15 November–5 January, 1914.
579. Bas-relief
580. Buste (plâtre)
581. Sculptures, bas-reliefs et architecture faisant partie de l'ensemble Mare.

———

André Mare
1432. Petite Salon. Avec la collaboration de Duchamp-Villon, R. de la Fresnaye, R. Desvallières, M. Marinot, Vallois.

Gand. Exposition Universelle et Internationale de Gand. Groupe II.
Beaux-Arts, oeuvres modernes
462. Jeune fille, statue terre cuite

1914
Prague. Mánes Fine Arts Society. February–March. Introduction by Alexander Mercereau. Included Bruce, Delaunay, de la Fresnaye,

Gleizes, Lhote, Marchand, Metzinger, Mondrian, Villon, Archipenko and Brancusi.
125. Lovers. Bas-relief. Plaster
126. Baudelaire. Bronze
127. Torso. Terracotta
128. Little dancers. Terracotta
129. Vase. Terracotta
130. Cat. Plaster

Galerie André Groult. 6 April–3 May. Exposition de sculptures de R. Duchamp-Villon, Aquarelles d'Albert Gleizes, Gravures de Jacques Villon, Dessins de Jean Metzinger. Preface by André Salmon.
1. Vieux Paysan. Buste pierre. 1907
2. Visage d'enfant. Cire perdu. 1908
3. Portrait de jeune fille. Bronze, appart. à M.E.D. 1908
4. Chanson. Groupe bois. 1908
5. Jeune fille assise. Terre cuite. 1909
6. Torso de femme. Terre cuite. 1910
7. Torse d'homme. Terre cuite. 1910
8. Petits danseurs. Terre cuite. 1911
9. Vasque décorative. Pierre. 1911
10. Baudelaire. Terre cuite. 1911
11. Esquisse pour Baudelaire. Bronze. 1911
12. Idem
13. Visage de femme. Terre cuite. Art. à G.R.D. 1912
14. Les Amants. Bas relief. Terre cuite. 1913
15. Esquisse pour Les Amants. Plâtre. Art. à l'auteur. 1913
16. "Le Chat." Medallion bois. 1913
17. "Le Perroquet." Idem. 1913
18. "Le Chien." Esquisse terre cuite. 1913
19. Femme assise. Bronze. 1914
20. Projet pour une statue. Plâtre. 1914
21. Portrait. Buste plâtre. 1914
Architecture
22. Étude pour une balcon. 1912
23. Idem
24. Idem
25. Idem
26. Vasque décorative pour un jardin. 1913
27. Maquette pour un fronton. Terre cuite. 1912
27 bis. Projet d'hôtel (photo). 1912

Berlin. Der Sturm. June–July. With Gleizes, Metzinger, Villon.
1915
New York. Carroll Galleries. "Second Exhibition of Works by Contemporary French Artists." February.

29. Lovers. Bas-relief
30. Woman Seated. Sculpture
31. Parrot. Bas-relief
32. Cat. Bas-relief

1917
New York. Society of Independent Artists. April–May
108. Torse
109. Architectural Sculpture

1919
Salon d'Automne. 1 November–10 December.
542. Esope. 1906
543. Vieux Paysan. 1907
544. Chanson. 1908
545. Portrait de Jeune Fille. 1908
546. Jeune fille assise. 1909
547. Pastorale (fragment). 1910
548. Nymphe de Bois. 1911
549. Baudelaire. 1911
550. Vasque décorative. 1911
551. Projet d'Hôtel (photographie). 1912
552. Bas-relief. Les amants. 1913
553. Bas-relief. Le Chat. 1913
554. Bas-relief. Le Chien. 1913
555. Bas-relief. Les Pigeons. 1913
556. Buste. 1913
557. Femme assise. 1914
558. Le Coq
559. Bas-relief. Les petits danseurs
559 bis. Portrait du Professor Gosset (étude plâtre)

1925
Exposition de la Section d'Or: 1912–1925. Galerie Vavin-Raspail. January 12–31.
11. Portrait de Madame G.R.-D. 1912
12. Maquette pour le Portrait de Madame G.R.-D. 1912
13. Le Cheval. 1914
14. Les petits danseurs. Bronze. 1914
15. *Le Coq*. Bronze. 1916

1926
New York. The Art Center Exhibition of the Quinn Collection. January 7–30.
Torse d'homme
Baudelaire
Seated Woman

Salon des Indépendants. Trente Ans d'Art Indépendant. Exposition Rétrospective. Expositions Posthumes. 20 February–21 March.

Fig. 77 *Seated Woman*. Charcoal, 24³⁄₁₆ × 18¾ in. Musée des Beaux-Arts de Rouen

2928. Chanson (sculpture bois) 1908
2929. Torse d'homme (terre cuitre) 1910
2930. Baudelaire (terre cuite) 1911
2931. Vasque (pierre) 1911
2932. Les amants (bas-relief) 1913
2933. Cheval. 1914

Brooklyn. Brooklyn Academy of Arts and Sciences. Société Anonyme. International Exhibition of Modern Art. November 1–January 1, 1927.
Seated Woman

1927
New York. Société Anonyme. International Exhibition of Modern Art. Anderson Galleries. January 25–February 5.
Seated Woman
The Parrot

1929

New York. Brummer Gallery. Memorial Exhibition of the Works of Raymond Duchamp-Villon. January 5–February 9.

Plaster

1. Torso
2. Yvonne
3. Pastoral
4. Portrait of Maggy
5. Dog
6. Cat
7. Doves
8. Little Dancers
9. Horse
10. Study of Horse
11. Professor Gosset
12. Cock
13. Étude
14. Yvonne
15. Face of Young Man
16. Face of Young Girl
17. Head of Horse
18. Étude—Esope
19. Lady with Rooster
20. Madelaine
21. Woman Dancing
22. Étude—bas-relief
23. Étude—The Lovers
24. Étude
25. Étude

Terra-Cotta

26. Esope
27. Young Girl Seated
28. Male Torso
29. Baudelaire
30. Daughter of the Winds
31. Little Dancers
32. Housefront

Marble

33. La Liseuse

Stone

34. Aged Peasant
35. Vasque

Bronze

36. Étude—Maggy
37. Cock
38. Football

Cement

39. The Lovers

Wood

40. Song

Wax

41. Professor Gosset
42. Head of Horse
43. Small Head of Baudelaire
44. Maggy

Clay

45. Étude

Drawings

1931

Galerie Pierre. June 8–27.

1. Étude pour la femme au coq. Bronze 1907
2. Visage d'enfant. Bronze 1908
3. Tête d'enfant. Bronze 1908
4. Petit masque d'enfant. Bronze 1908
5. Étude pour la Pastorale. Bronze 1910
6. Mouvement de Danse. Bronze 1910
7. Torse d'homme. Terre cuite 1910
8. Baudelaire (Musée du Luxembourg). Bronze 1911
9. Baudelaire (étude). Petit Bronze 1911
10. Baudelaire (étude). Petit Bronze 1911
11. La Vasque (fragment). Bronze 1911
12. Esquisse pour la Vasque. Petit Bronze 1911
13. Maggy. Bronze 1912
14. Architecture. Photographie 1912
15. Les Amants (Musée du Luxembourg). Plâtre 1913
16. Les Amants, 1re étude. Bronze 1913
17. Les Amants, 2e étude. Bronze 1913
18. Les Amants, 3e étude. Bronze 1913
19. Les Amants, 4e étude. Bronze 1913
20. Le chat. Bronze 1913
21. La femme assise. Bronze 1914
22. Petits danseurs. Bronze 1914
23. LE CHEVAL. Bronze 1914
24. Le cavalier droit. Bronze 1914
25. Le cavalier penché. Bronze 1914
26. Étude de cheval. Bronze 1914
27. Tête de cheval. Bronze 1914
28. Étude pour tête de cheval. Bronze 1914
29. Petit cheval. Bronze 1914
30. Autre petit cheval. Bronze 1914
31. Jeune fille assise. Plâtre 1914
32. Portrait du Professeur Gosset. Bronze 1917
33. Le coq. Plâtre 1917

Galerie Dru, Bourgeat et Van Gelder. Peintures, gouaches, et pastels de Charles Dufresne. Sculptures de Duchamp-Villon. Preface by Walter Pach.

Torse d'homme
Tête de Baudelaire
Tête de jeune fille
Vasque

1942

Galerie de France. March 7–20. With his brothers.

1. Torse de jeune homme. 1910
2. Baudelaire. 1911
3. La Danse.
4. Magda. 1912
5. Les Amants. 1913
6. Le Cheval. 1914
7. La femme assise. 1914

1945
New Haven. Yale University Art Gallery. March. With his brothers.

1967
New York. Solomon R. Guggenheim Museum. January 8–February 17. With his brothers.

1963
Galerie Louis Carré. June 17–July 20

1966
Galerie Louis Carré. Le Cheval Majeur. June 23–December 24

1967
Rouen. Musée de Rouen. Les Duchamps. April 15–June 1

Musée National d'Art Moderne. Raymond Duchamp-Villon. Marcel Duchamp. June 7–July 2

Fig. 79   *Seated Woman*. Charcoal, 18⅞ × 12⅜ in. Musée National d'Art Moderne, Paris